Collecting Everyday Miracles

Commit to Being Empowered

JEN WARD

Copyright © 2018 Jen Ward

All rights reserved. No part of this book may be reproduced, stored in a retrieval system, or transmitted in any form by any means without written permission of the author.

ISBN-13: 978-0-9994954-3-8 for print version

JEN WARD

Healing happens in the fertile ground of receptiveness, openness and kindness. Issues occur to stretch our capacity to embrace the Miraculous Universe. Those of us who see miracles in all places are able to facilitate those miracles working in the lives of others. Yet there must be a level of openness as a starting point.

That is why everyone who believes in healing is right and everyone who doesn't believe in healing is right. Because it does depend on the person's receptivity.

- Jen Ward

CONTENTS

	Introduction	1
1	Homage to You	4
2	The Alchemy of Lives	5
3	Misnomers About Spirituality	6
4	The Truth About Truth	11
5	The Dance of Questions and Answers	14
6	How to Be Spiritual	18
7	The Shift	20
8	The Truth About Pain	23
9	How Women Dilute Their Effectiveness	29
10	Checklist for Self Worth	32
11	Checklist for Friendship	34
12	Checklist to Reduce Pain	37
13	Prayer	39
14	How to Deal with Judgmental People	40
15	How to Nurture Your Individuality	41
16	How to Live Your Purpose	46
17	How to Finish a Project	49
18	How to Get Your Miracle	52
19	How to Transcend	53
20	The Wonder of Life	57

21	Ways to Open Up Your Energy Field	59
22	How to Connect with Your Spirit Guides	62
23	Connect With Your Guides	67
24	Upgrades in Spiritual Belief System in the Fifth Dimension	68
25	Stay Closed to Psychic Intrusion	73
26	Reasons People Are Not Free	75
27	I Stand By My Convictions	78
28	I Am Alone Today	79
29	You Know That Excruciating Loneliness	83
30	How to Use Speech to Empower Yourself	84
31	The Quickest Route to Transcendence	88
32	What Aware Souls Do	94
33	How to Bless Someone	99
34	The Stillness of the Pond	101
35	Ways Your Pet Is Healing	103
36	How to Raise Your Furry Family's Self Esteem	105
37	How to Be a Good Listener	108
38	An Extension of Our Own Beingness	112
39	Don't Waste Energy	115
40	Stop the Madness	119
41	Important Facts About Trees	122
42	Ways to Shut Down Your Energy Field	127
43	What Is Causing Your Mood?	130

44	Ways We Curse Others	133
45	How to Say F#@k You to Someone	135
46	Words and Phrases That Should Be Retired	140
47	How to Remove Yourself from Linear Limitations	144
48	If You Think Life Is Throwing Everything It Can at You	149
49	Respecting Inanimate Life: The Secret to Having	150
50	Things To Know When a Loved One Is Ready to Cross Over	153
51	How Adopting Reincarnation Universally Will Save the World	160
52	Message from Your Heart	164
	About the Author	167
	Other Books by Jen Ward	169

INTRODUCTION

I am here to help people with the upgrade and remove themselves from linear enslavement. It is what we are witnessing everyone break free of right now. Linear existence has been the way to enslave the masses. It has squelched creativity and self-empowerment.

Individuals have diluted their effectiveness by donating it to fortify groups. These are the same groups that diminish us. The fix is to withdraw all our energy from groups and to regain our individual empowerment. It is like taking the foundation out of power structures little by little until they crumble of their own accord.

This is also what we are witnessing. It seems scary. But it is necessary for humanity to recalibrate to respecting individuality and returning reverence back to life. Individuals have been diluted and leeched of all of their good qualities. It is a kind of human fracking.

Since I have such an understanding of energy, I am assisting the people who do the taps I post in how to take back their essence from the power structures and regain their personal integrity. Along with that, people need to adopt a better way of treating each other so there is some education in that department too.

We have been pitted against each other and used to diminish ourselves to benefit an ignoble intention. An example of that is black on black crimes. This is done by infusing mainly black neighborhoods with easy access drugs and handguns which keeps people in defense mode more readily than allowing them to focus on a better quality of life.

The more people who awaken to what is necessary in taking back our empowerment from groups, the more quickly we can regain our humanity. The more people who have the luxury of understanding this because they are not immersed in survival mode, the more this awareness can awaken the masses.

The more people who do the taps I post with the intention of assisting others who aren't able to assist themselves yet in this way, the greater immediate impact we will have on the consciousness of the planet.

Collecting Everyday Miracles

1 HOMAGE TO YOU

You are as fluid as an ocean

More expansive than the sky

As determined as an echo

More breathless than a sigh

Astonishing as a windpipe dream

That meets its manifestation

As pure as the providence of soul

At its final destination

You are a Joyful Whisper

Completed in a smile

The perfect pair of stylish shoes

That can go the extra mile

You are divinity personified

That leaves no doubt, no less

Where alpha and omega meet

Is you, humanly expressed.

2 THE ALCHEMY OF LIVES

Kindness, resolve and a sense of Peace are a reflection of who we are as spiritual beings. Our work and home lives are the point of entry that showcase our spiritual state to all who are privy to us. Converting the chaos that embodies the physical realm into Joy, Love, Abundance, Freedom for all is the spiritual alchemy that is spinning straw into Gold. How we use our gifts to uplift and enlighten others is where the "rubber meets the road."

3 MISNOMERS ABOUT SPIRITUALITY

It is important to seek perfection. Actually, it is important to manifest your individuality. There is no such thing as perfection in the physical realm. Fully embracing your uniqueness is a means of breaking out of the mold of linear existence. Instead of being a stick figure on a linear conveyor belt, you are a starburst with unlimited possibilities and potential.

It is important to be good. That was a moral code enacted by man. It is important to listen to your own instincts in regards to right action, speech and living. Being good may be veering in the opposite direction of being real. Enlightenment doesn't happen through being good. Enlightenment happens by venturing through the terrifying aspects of yourself until you push through them and see the illusion of them.

You should be afraid of helping someone because you can take on their karma. The fear in taking on karma itself is setting you up not to reach your potential. Love is the opposite of fear so if you are afraid of anything, you are at a lesser vantage point than pure love. Being pure love is the goal. You can only take on karma from working at a limited vantage point of a body.

You are not a physical body if you are working in energy. You are an energy field. You can expand your consciousness to be as big as your mind and heart can fathom. So if you do allow energy to pass through your system to release, make your energy field as big as a galaxy and move the energy to the other side of yourself and dilute and dissipate it. It is that kind of awareness that keeps any stagnant energy from pouring into your physicality.

Keep the vibration of yourself as an energy being at such a high frequency that whatever is released does not resonate with you in the microcosm and it is easily dissipated. Fear DROPS your vibration and is counter indicated to assisting.

You need to be helped by someone outside of yourself. There are Guides and helpers every step of the way. As soon as you give allegiance to an outside Source, you are veering away from your own potential. Outer sources are merely guideposts to direct you back to adhering to you own inner compass. It is up to you and well within your means to tap into direct truth yourself.

That God is a force outside of you. That is the belief that has kept a whole ocean of droplets of water from realizing they are the ocean themselves. A droplet of water is a microcosm of the great ocean. In this way, you are a microcosm of God. If a water droplet tried to taint other water droplets, it would be tainting an aspect of itself in the macrocosm. When people hate, judge and diminish others, they are tainting their own macrocosm. It is that simple. To dishonor any other beings is a limitation to your own omnipotence. Those who discredit others show a lack of awareness of their own essence.

It is good to be humble. Humility as it is taught to the masses is wrong. It has been a means to control all of humanity by having them abase themselves. True humility is seeing the same potential in others as you see in yourself. It is irrelevant what level that is. If you believe you are the most amazing being on the planet, that can still be humility as long as you see every other being as the most amazing being on the planet as well. Thinking that you need to debase yourself to be humble merely lowers the bar on all of humanity.

You should send your energy up to the sky when you pray. We were taught to do this as a means of dissipating our own energy as individuals and as a group. That is why churches have steeples and we point our hands up into the sky when we are most reverent in energy. They are like divining rods to send the energy up and out of us. We would be more empowered to pour the energy within ourselves because God is within. This would make us all stronger, empowered and omniscient beings which is a great way to pay homage to Source.

The word God is a man made concept because language is a tool of man. God does not need to be draped in words, praise or devotion to sustain itself. This is man's need. Man is not made in God's image, God was made in man's flawed image which is very limited. The world is in such a mess because of man's limited concept of God. Man himself is flawed and projects all those flaws onto Source.

It is better to be poor to be Godly. Money is energy. A spiritual person is able to appreciate and handle energy in all forms, even money. But being obsessed with the notion of being rich is like abiding by a clock where only noon and midnight count. Monetary wealth is only one form of abundance. To focus too much importance on it is to miss so much of life for the obsession.

There is a hell outside of our own making. Gratitude is the precipice of heaven because it opens up all the energy systems in the body to accept more love, light and blessings. As gratitude is the precipice of heaven, regret is the doorway to hell. It closes down energy systems and leaves the person trapped in a very narrow band of consciousness. If someone is filled with regret, they are indeed trapped in a hell of their own making.

Meditation is a means to transcendence. Meditation can only take you to the mental realms. The mental realms also house the ego. The mental realms can not get you into the pure positive realms of spirit just like a ladder can only get you to the top of the roof but can't immerse you in the total freedom of the sky. To transcend, you must awaken all your subtle senses and not only rely on the ones that we are familiar with in our linear perceptions. The best way to do this is to shift from meditation to enhancing all the senses through visualizations. This is actually coming from the heart instead of the mind. It is done by utilizing creativity, imagination and childlike exuberance. One can still call it meditation, but it is more of an enhanced experience. When one has gotten to the top of the mental realms, their ego will conjure up terrifying threats of dying. This is actually the ego afraid of being killed off if you continue your quest and using fear of dying to shut you down. It has been an effective tool to do this. But now we know the ruse.

Getting out of the body is important to your spirituality. Many people feel like a failure because they can't achieve out of body experiences. But it is not necessary. What is more valuable is learning to stay in your center and seeing yourself as the center point of the Universe. Allow all life to orbit around you. That is how to stay empowered. And instead of needing to leave your body, you need merely to expand all your atoms to expand your awareness and perceive anywhere in the Universe from your center.

It is important to belong to a group. Spirituality is a process of taking back all your energy from any person or group who has used you for an energy source for their intention. That is what is happening in the world right now as so many are being disillusioned by the lack of authority in groups. Groups have lost their ability to deceive us. The illusion is being stripped off and with it, their effectiveness to deceive and enslave us. Once you remove all your energy from everyone and everything, it is then that it can be innately used to EMPOWER everyone and everything with you at the helm. You must never be left out of the equation.

4 THE TRUTH ABOUT TRUTH

The world is starving for truth, NOT Bullies.

Although truth can seem harsh because it is ripping off comfortable layers of lies, it does not destroy.

It can hurt the feelings, but the feelings are very low on the survival scale.

Truth resonates similarly to love.

The reason there is so little love in the world is because there is so little truth in the world.

Being a bully is not being loving.

Administering truth to those with an aversion to it is intricate work.

It is energetic surgery.

One must know how much truth to administer without cutting too deep. It takes precision.

Being polite but secretly dreading is not truth.

Being nice to someone but talking behind their back is not truthful or loving.

Talking about anyone is not truth.

Complaints are not truth.

Gossip is not truth.

Judgment is ignorant lies.

Ignorant because the one judging believes they know the absolute truth.

Silence, Love and Joy are the only absolute truths.

Judgment is merely a vantage point.

Labels are not truth. They are nailing things in a fixed state.

Life is expansive. Truth reflects this.

The best depiction of truth is silence.

This is why Native Americans have used sign language.

They honor truth in this way.

God does not need to be praised, worshiped or have an ego stroked.

God has no ego.

If one wants to honor God, one can speak truth.

The greatest truth is silence.

Truth is showing reverence for God.

If God is love

And Love and truth resonate similarly,

And being silent resonates with truth

Then being silent is being in the presence of God.

This is how to honor God.

As you speak, notice how much of it is not necessary.

Notice how much it does not resonate with truth.

If it does not resonate with truth, it does not resonate with God.

Notice how much you speak of negative things.

Notice how much you talk to hide who you are.

Notice how much you talk about others.

Notice how much you talk about yourself.

If you could cut away all of that chatter, you could feel more clearly the depth of your own soul.

You would be able to truly honor God in that silence.

For in silence you express the absolute truth.

Silence is truth, love and awareness combined.

When you are silent in your words and thoughts,

You are truly being truthful.

You resonate with God.

5 THE DANCE OF QUESTIONS AND ANSWERS

Who will I help?

How will I serve?

What will I do to add more kindness to the world?

How can I honor myself more?

How can I bring more honor to someone else?

How will I express Love in a different way today?

What are the little miracles?

What secrets does the stillness hold?

What gifts have I been withholding that I am ready to share?

What are those little blind spots in me?

How do I release them?

Am I ready to release them?

Do they make me feel special?

Why do I need to feel special?

What craving in me does validation satiate?

Can I fill it myself?

Can I feed myself the succor of life?

What answers do I have that I have overlooked?

Who really understands me?

Do I really understand myself?

Am I worthy?

What makes me worthy?

Is everybody worthy?

What would disqualify someone from being worthy?

Is it obedience?

What atrocities may they have endured to remove them from appearing loving?

Is it my place to inflict more upon them?

How much does one judgment weigh?

How many judgments does it take to weigh down a soul?

Who benefits when a soul gets discouraged?

How many tears are cried at the judgment of and indifference to others?

Is it easier to inflict pain or endure it?

Is my pain self-induced?

How many degrees of separation are there between a transgression and its reciprocation?

How much of what I endure have I agreed to?

How many teachers and Guides do I have?

Am I awake now or when I sleep?

What does it take to be and stay awake in both?

How many others think such thoughts?

Am I alone in my quest for answers?

Am I different?

Or, is everyone pondering how to get out of the cell of human consciousness in their cell as well?

Can we be free as individuals?

Can we make a mass escape?

Where is the key hidden?

How do I slip it to the others?

How will we recognize we are free?

How will we know truth when we finally perceive it?

Does it really matter?

Do I really matter?

Am I having the same thoughts as any random cell in a vast array of matter?

Does everyone matter?

Yes. Yes they do. Yes they think, feel and struggle alone and believe it isolates them greatly. It creates such angst in them. They do not realize that this anguish to be better, fulfilled and empowered is the connecting force with all of life.

We are connected in this struggle. Reach out through those questions to tentative hearts everywhere.

Use them as intangible fingers to wipe the brow of the more weary,

To hug the ones that feel more alone,

To feed the hearts of those who are more depleted,

To awaken those who are more asleep,

To nurture those who are more depraved,

To expand the consciousness of Life by giving, in all ways, to all beings and in all moments.

You are this capable.

Enjoy your day and all the internal questions and answers that dance within you.

May your intentions inspire others to dance.

You are loved and appreciated

In, and by, All.

6 HOW TO BE SPIRITUAL

Realize that you are much more than a physical body.

Forgo getting caught up in emotional drama. Realize that emotions are an escape valve for stagnant energy or a sensory system to gauge when you are coming out of alignment. They are not meant as a form of entertainment, manipulation or distraction.

Realize that there is a goal beyond the mind. The mind exists at the same level as the ego. So the ego works against transcending the mind. It is important to understand what one is dealing with in the intention of transcending.

Understand that judging others is merely a distraction from working on your own self. It is a form of denial.

Forgo indulging in the future or the past. Your empowerment exists in the moment, and the more you indulge in the past or present, the more you dilute your own effectiveness.

Bow out of politics and religion. Both have been become gangrene on the toe of humanity.

Realize God doesn't have a gender.

Trust in your own omniscience. You never die. Life is a continuation of experiences. We accrue every possible scenario of existence so as to have compassion for all life. If you don't have a reference point for a particular experience, it is because you never experienced something like that or it is so painful that you block it out as a form of denial.

Stop taking sides in the rhetoric of life. The manipulators of situations use your energy to fuel division. Learn from those family dynamics that are so exasperating.

Worry less about being good and focus more on holding a space for truth. Truth and love resonate similarly. If you focus more on being truthful and loving, you will discover many more of the secrets withheld from those who compartmentalize life.

Honor, respect and listen to all life. This includes all atoms of life. Humans are not superior in importance. This belief is their own limitation to overcome. Wisdom is held in the ability to connect in energy to all animals, plants, trees, even sacred stones and ALL inanimate life as well. All life is speaking to you. It is a matter of tuning in to listen.

Forgo all self-deprecation. This includes feeling unworthy and false humility. True humility is a practice of honoring all life. It has been used as a means to self-subjugate.

Practice Love, gratitude and truth in all ways. The more painful it is to expose your own failings, the freer your true self will be.

7 THE SHIFT

In past lives:

- we were called out for speaking our mind,
- tortured for being strong willed,
- deemed a criminal for being literate,
- sacrificed for being pure,
- treated like property for being beautiful,
- pitted against each other for being strong,
- excommunicated for communing with God,
- called a heathen for communing with nature,
- called lazy or flaky for wanting peace,
- shot for desertion for running from war,
- put into slavery for the color of our skin,
- demoralized for whom we loved,
- preached to that money was evil,
- born to people who hate us....

No wonder people have cringed within a corner of their own energy field and are afraid of their own empowerment.

It is time to:

- Be beautifully bold,
- Speak our truth,
- Value wisdom,
- Pull away from the pack,
- Give homage to the God of one's choosing, the one that empowers them to love,
- Love in a rainbow of diversity,
- Embrace freedom,
- See the cleanliness of being filthy rich,
- Reject conformity,
- Unfurl one's wings,
- Dance on a whim,
- Speak one's heart,
- Honor the greatness in each other,
- Empower All,
- Strip the illusion off the power mongers,
- Walk all over their puny insignificance,
- Take our power back,

- Redistribute power to the individuals who are still scratching their head,
- Enliven hope,
- Enliven wonder,
- Enliven the world,
- Hug a forest!
- Be vulnerable,
- Express virtue,
- Speak of Love,
- Be demonstrative in loving life,
- Live our purpose,
- Share our dreams,
- Nurture kindness,
- Teach in a million ways,
- Speak in a million tongues,
- Readopt a simpler lifestyle,
- See beauty in its true form,
- Forgo dis-ease,
- Uplift consciousness,
- Awaken in the spirit of love!

8 THE TRUTH ABOUT PAIN

What many people don't realize is that many times when their body is feeling pain, it is an issue moving OUT of the body. Humans have been so conditioned to think of themselves as merely linear beings moving in one direction. This is such a disservice to them.

Energy can move in all directions. To see life as being on a conveyor belt of time moving towards an ultimate degeneration and death is merely a way of manifesting that horrible reality. Your mind is a 3D printer so if that is what you believe, that is what you will create.

Issues are clouds of energy that have superimposed your energy. That is why the pain moves around. That is why doctors can only diagnose the effects of it and not what causes it. You are only terminal as long as you are on the linear conveyor belt. In all other measurements of reality, you are exponentially expansive. You are not such a solid form, but a starburst.

The thing that holds an issue in the body is identifying with it. So as soon as you get a diagnosis, you OWN that issue. I am so surprised by so many people's pride in sharing their issues. It is as if it validates them in some way. Maybe when they were a child they got special treatment for being sick. That is the primal experience that plays out when people share their diagnosis freely.

When there is an issue in the body, think of all the different traumas that could have been stored in one's DNA.

- Hanging and decapitations on the neck.

- Being a slave and carrying the burdens of another for the back.

- Praying to an indifferent God for the knees.

- Migrating over hot stones for the feet.

- Being forced from a home that you love would create a weary spirit.

- Losing a loved one to an early death could bring apathy and depression.

- Being forced to fight for a ruthless king in the name of God could cause one easily to become an atheist.

- Being forced to fight to the death would cause someone to not want to defend themselves.

- Abusing power would cause someone to feel such guilt that they now deem themselves unworthy.

These are some of the many issues that we store in our DNA from our ancestors. Man has been the most ruthless beast. They are the only beings that have taken pleasure from inflicting pain. They are the only beings that use pain as an identification marker when meeting and interacting with others. Every other being wants to appear empowered. Man is the only being that is so broken by the treatment from other men that he prefers to define himself as diseased or flawed rather than show up whole.

All these issues are trying to move out of your body to make you whole and empowered. But we stop that process by holding onto them and owning the pain they cause. If the pain were an issue coming to the surface to release, your talking about it would be the belt to secure it nicely to your body.

Why not try another way? Why not see the issues as something moving through your very fluid body? If they get stuck in an area, imagine shaking them loose and allowing them to slip away. You can still enjoy your western medications as you do this. Just don't allow anyone to crown you with a label of disease as if it were a prize you won by default. It is not. You are pure and perfect. What a better position to hold.

Here are some of the taps to specifically address pain:

(Say each statement three times out loud while tapping on your head and say it a fourth time while tapping on your chest.)

"I release being at the mercy of pain; in all moments."

"I release giving pain my power; in all moments."

"I release using pain to validate myself; in all moments."

"I release using pain as a crutch; in all moments."

"I release being enslaved to pain; in all moments."

"I release using pain as an excuse; in all moments."

"I release using pain to feel important; in all moments."

"I release using pain to punish myself; in all moments."

"I release using pain to declare myself unworthy; in all moments."

"I release the belief that pain is omniscient; in all moments."

"I release the belief that pain is omnipresent; in all moments."

"I release the belief that pain is omnipotent; in all moments."

"I release worshiping pain; in all moments."

"I release being trapped in hell; in all moments."

"I release converting hell into pain; in all moments."

"I release using pain to express being in hell; in all moments."

"I release making a God out of pain; in all moments."

"I release storing hell in my nerve endings; in all moments."

"I recant all vows and agreements between myself and pain; in all moments."

"I remove all curses between myself and pain; in all moments."

"I sever all strings and cords between myself and all pain; in all moments."

"I dissolve all karmic ties between myself and pain; in all moments."

"I sever all strings and cords between myself and my pain body; in all moments."

"I step out of my pain body and disintegrate it; in all moments."

"I remove all the pain, burden, limitations and engrams that pain has put on me; in all moments."

"I take back all the joy, love, abundance, freedom, health success, security, companionship, creativity, peace, life, wholeness, beauty, enthusiasm, contentment, spirituality, enlightenment and confidence that pain has taken from me; in all moments."

"I release being permeated in pain; in all moments."

"I withdraw all my energy from pain; in all moments."

"I annihilate all concepts of pain; in all moments."

"I annihilate all memories of pain; in all moments."

"I annihilate all feelings of pain; in all moments."

"I annihilate all physical components of pain; in all moments."

"I convert all pain to a joyous expression of gratitude; in all moments."

"I release resonating with pain; in all moments."

"I release emanating with pain; in all moments."

"I remove all pain from my sound frequency; in all moments."

"I remove all pain from my light body; in all moments."

"I shift my paradigm from pain to joy, love, abundance, freedom, health, success, security, companionship, creativity, peace, life, wholeness, beauty, enthusiasm, contentment, spirituality, enlightenment and confidence; in all moments."

"I transcend pain; in all moments."

"I am centered and empowered in Divine Love; in all moments."

"I resonate and emanate Divine Love; in all moments."

9 HOW WOMEN DILUTE THEIR EFFECTIVENESS

Wearing synthetic clothing. This is like wrapping one's energy system in cellophane.

Wearing high heel shoes all the time. The feet are meant to connect their energy into the ground. It is a way of communication. Wearing high heels is a means of keeping female empowerment less balanced.

Cutting their hair. Hair is like tiny antennas. Cutting it all off is a means of cutting her off from subtle perception.

Imitating male energy rather than being authentically female. That means competing with other women, wearing make up like war paint and being driven in a way that male energy is driven.

Adopting a deference to men which is conditioned into most societies these days. This means mistrusting their innate gut feelings and deferring to the most powerful outer voices even if they are clearly abusive and imbalanced.

Becoming wives and mothers out of obligation and not because it is something they desire to do.

Participating in social activities out of obligation.

Defining themselves by how much they nurture others.

Forgoing their own dreams and desires to make everyone else happy.

Worrying more about being polite or being considered a good person than how to stay centered.

Competing with other women instead of supporting them in the spirit of sisterhood.

Wasting energy complaining, gossiping or talking too much.

Giving form to negative things through what they put attention on.

Cursing others by deeming them sad.

Dumbing individuals down a level through comparison.

Wasting energy with concern in other people's business through being judgmental.

Obsessing over physical beauty and their ability to attract a partner.

Waiting for a man to save them.

Lamenting over not attracting the perfect life partner.

Belittling the life partner that they currently have.

Perpetuating a belief system ingrained with male superiority.

Worshiping a God that is fear based and shaming rather than nurturing and encouraging.

Putting themselves down or being self-diminishing in any way.

Believing that they are unworthy in some way.

Adopting the rhetoric or behavior of their men folk.

Taking up causes in a way that feeds the negative aspect of themselves rather than dissipates it.

Forgetting that they are Goddess personified.

10 CHECKLIST FOR SELF-WORTH

- Stop making jokes at your own expense.

- Stop comparing yourself to others.

- Take time, when you think of it, to say thank you to aspects of yourself. For example, if you are running, thank your legs and heart for their service.

- When someone says something nice about you, don't push it away.

- Don't make excuses for yourself in your head ready to give out if confronted. You don't have to defend your being. You deserve to exist. You are a wonder.

- Take in the compliments and the kindness. They are energy that is sustenance.

- When you enter a room, have the intention that you benefit everyone with your presence. Then give out goodwill to all.

- Imagine yourself engulfed in a sunburst of love that everyone who engages you gets to benefit from.

- Accept your uniqueness not as a flaw but as an accent on your individuality.

- Be proud of the package that you are in.

- Don't berate yourself if you are not happy with your attributes. Every aspect of you is giving a hundred percent to you. Stop belittling your aspects unnecessarily.

- Instead of trying to be like others, embrace the way you are different.

- Stop wanting aspects of yourself to look or be like others. If you like others' attributes, enjoy them on others but embrace your own as you.

- Never put the glass ceiling on yourself that family members struggle with. If someone in the family has an issue, it doesn't mean you will just because you are related.

- If you have children, the way you treat yourself will imprint on them. If you sacrifice everything for your children, you are teaching them to be martyrs.

- If you want your partner to respect you, respect yourself. Your confidence is attractive. Being a doormat is not.

- Communicate your wishes clearly and without drama. People respect simple uncomplicated interaction.

- Stop living out the dreams and wishes of another simply because you are afraid to tell them what you really want. This is your life experience, not theirs.

- Do what you love to do. This will make all the cells of your body happy.

- Dare to be different. It is what makes you special.

11 CHECKLIST FOR FRIENDSHIP

- Always be truthful.

- Don't do things you secretly resent (that is not truthful).

- Friendship is not a dumping service. This is using each other. If it is done continually, you are just smearing around the issues and muddling the relationship.

- Stroking the ego is manipulative, not genuine. It gets old.

- Enabling is using someone for a crutch. It is not friendship to dis-empower someone.

- A friend should have the same code of ethics as a therapist. If something is shared, it is not fodder for conversation ever.

- Pitting friends against each other is playing some kind of competitive game. One should be able to relax around friends, not be in defense mode.

- Sharing the same dysfunction is not friendship if one is using the other to stay dysfunctional. Friends see the best in each other; they don't use each other as an excuse or a means to get a fix.

- If gossip or complaining (venting) is your connection, it is keeping you immersed in a very low vibration. They are dysfunctions.

- Insults, criticism and passive aggressive remarks are not for friends. They are for adversaries, if at all.

- Friends see the best in each other and bring that out.

- There is no need for competition. This is displaying past lives of rivalry and you may be connected out of habit.

- Friends make each other feel better. If one is always feeling better than another, then the other is being used in a sense.

- Being a friend is not an easy pass to diminish another in any way. The line, "I don't want to see you get hurt" precludes something that is hurtful.

- Friends support, nurture, and uplift each other. They don't use the other to feel better about themselves, feel entitled to squelch a person's dreams or to limit them in any way.

- Friends have clear boundaries when it comes to whom the other person is dating. If you are uncomfortable with your friend being around your partner, then there is probably a reason. Friends are beyond reproach.

- When we maintain a certain standard for what we allow in our lives and how we will be treated, we train others around us how to be treated.

- Pay attention to your actions because they speak louder than words. You are forging your resume of self-respect as you respect others.

- A friend is someone you can relax your atoms around. If you feel like you are defensive or compromised in any way being around someone, it isn't worth the price of being uncomfortable in your skin.

- The fear of being alone should not be the reason to be friends. The one thing worse than being alone is being used.

- You can never lose the amount of love you have right now. If you must let go of someone because it does not better you to be around them, let them go. Once you create that vacuum, the Universe will fill it with someone more suited to enhance your intention to be a better person.

- You should be your very best friend. Never diminish, debase, or dilute your empowerment to serve the needs of another. If you give service and sacrifice out of love, it is never diminishing, debasing or dis-empowering.

12 CHECKLIST TO REDUCE PAIN

So many are in chronic pain. Here is a checklist to help you uncover the tipping point for yourself. The environment has gotten so toxic that it is not enough to just show up. For so many, this list is their lifeline to less pain.

- Soaks in Epsom salts and hydrogen peroxide.
- Take MSM.
- Only wear breathable clothes.
- Take all perfumes and dyes out of your diet.
- Go off white sugar and gluten.
- Use magnets, crystals and kelp to ground your energy.
- Remove all toxic people from your life.
- Use hypoallergenic products.
- Turn off the news.
- Take all nitrates and preservatives out of your diet.
- Do you spend time during the day doing something just for you?
- Do you spend time in nature?

- Do you do hobbies or things that bring you joy?

- Walk and stretch. It gets your lymphatic system moving.

- Nurture yourself.

- Get nurturing for yourself.

- Listen to, and/or sing uplifting music.

- Open your energy system often by being grateful.

- Eliminate all negative words and thoughts from your environment.

- Forgo talking about issues as if you own them or they define you.

- Forgo seeking negative attention or taking on the role of a victim.

- Listen to your gut.

- Stop trying to do it all.

- Forgo your schedule and drop out of time and space.

- Get enough rest.

- Forgo guilt.

- Listen to your body parts. Love them. They are starving for validation worse than the whole human is.

13 PRAYER

Prayer isn't something to do. Prayer is something to be.

When you:

- Allow others their voice
- Are kind
- Forego negative banter
- See the best in others
- Encourage, uplift and enlighten
- Speak truth in a kind way
- Take care of others
- Honor life in all forms
- Allow others the freedom to flourish
- Cheerlead for others
- Assist others in shining
- Challenge ways that diminish others
- Stop diminishing yourself
- Stop competing in a billion meaningless ways
- Are grateful for all the splendors of life

...then you are a living, breathing prayer.

14 HOW TO DEAL WITH JUDGMENTAL PEOPLE

It is hard not to be on the receiving end of judgment. Honesty has a similar vibration to love, so if you are honest as to how it makes you feel, you are being loving.

The best thing you can do is not to be around people who don't honor you.

Another thing to do is not share anything with someone who does this. If someone limits you in this way, say, "I am sorry, I thought I could trust you with what is important to me, I will not discuss it with you again." Then don't.

If they give their advice that you didn't ask for, say, "I am not asking your opinion or permission to be me."

Also, adopt a vantage point of seeing yourself at a different vantage point than them. If they are hurtful and unkind, see them as five year old children because that is what they are like spiritually. And who can be offended by a five year old?

15 HOW TO NURTURE YOUR INDIVIDUALITY

Stop being agreeable just to be agreeable. It doesn't earn you respect. It just assures that you will be overlooked more. There are some people who always get their way. They can be bullies about it. If you are agreeable because you don't want to upset them, then you are making it easier for them to bully others along the way. If you speak your truth in a gentle but firm way, it will be teaching the bullies and the blowhards that they will not self-destruct if every decision doesn't tilt in their favor. You can make it easier for those who can't so easily walk away from their relationship with this person.

Be unpredictable. If you do something regularly, study exactly why you do it that way. If it is because your parents always did it that way, that is not a good enough reason. Break those conditioning practices within yourself even if it seems uncomfortable.

Express your individuality in terms of personal style. If you are hesitant, try it out in subtle ways to get comfortable. These are not small changes. Individual choices are a means of defining yourself. Abiding by archaic mandates in style are a form of social slavery. Wear horizontal stripes if you like them. Wear white after Labor Day. Mix colors and patterns. If it disturbs others, you are freeing them of their conventional conditioning as well. Don't follow trends. Trends are a means to empower those who start them. They are evidence of how easily people follow. Not following trends is a means of breaking chains of conformity in a very non-threatening way.

Break up your routine. If you are used to being in front of the TV by a certain time, find another way of entertainment. Crumble the conditioning within yourself.

Don't agree to things you don't agree with. Your silence is perceived as complacency, or even worse, agreement. By saying nothing and going along with what is transpiring, you are energetically agreeing with it. It is a means of depleting yourself of any presence you may have had. If you don't agree with someone and are not able to speak up, it is very healthy to at least remove your energy from them so you are not misrepresented as being in agreement with them. They may be using your energy to strengthen their stance. To allow yourself to be used this way displays a total lack of self-respect. It dilutes your effectiveness.

Don't stay in a group that doesn't align with your beliefs just for the social aspect of it. Instead of forcing your family to go to a church that you have outgrown, find other ways to "force" the family bonding. Take classes together, find some hiking or camping or do gardening together, so you can all be in nature together.

Spending time in nature is the greatest way to hone your innate reverence. We all are, at the core, an aspect of nature.

Life is going to send you tests of integrity. The more you can define your own boundaries as to what you will and won't tolerate, the more you strengthen the stance of what you agree with in the world. When you agree with something, either consciously or inadvertently, you are creating more space for it in the world. Doing things just to fit in is a means of veering away from your own inner sense of self.

Stop celebrating events that mean nothing to you. Realize the core intention behind them to get a sense whether they align with your core values. If they do not, realize that may be the reason that your heart isn't into going through the motions of participating anymore.

Dust off all your own hobbies and the things you enjoy. They are all keys to your own empowerment. Whatever you naturally gravitate to is a means of revealing to yourself your natural abilities and passions. Natural abilities are talents thoroughly honed in past lives. The ability to paint may reveal a lifetime of studying as a starving artist with the great masters. Tapping into the things you enjoy doing is a means of tapping into the positive things that have happened in your past incarnations.

Break up your routine. Routine is like driving very cautiously in the slow lane. "Changing it up" is a means of merging onto the expressway and letting loose on the throttle.

Don't waste yourself by being around people just out of obligation. If you show up at family events just because you are expected to, when you are not valued and honored, then you are playing a cameo role in your own life. You are running lines for a bit part in someone else's major motion picture.

Drop out of time as much as possible. Time is a ruthless taskmaster. It will tell you that you must go to bed, stick to your routine and distract you from doing what you love. How many times has time commanded you to put your attention on work, problems and deadlines instead of your joy, love, abundance and freedom? There is a reason they are called deadlines. Because linear enslavement is a form of death.

Embrace the things that make you unique. Stop trying to be like everyone else. Those things that are different about you are the accents on your beauty. Sometimes you can observe someone who is considered very beautiful and then you can find all these flaws in them that drown out what seemed attractive at first. Someone who is not trapped in that initial impression has incredible freedom to be beautiful in multiple ways.

Realize that, for the most part, people are too busy being concerned about their own issues to fixate on yours. You are more free of their discernment than you realize. Anyone who fixates on your life is using you as a means of distracting from their own. Don't allow yourself to be used in this way by playing along with their expectations of you. This is a means of self-inflicted dysfunction.

Stop seeking the validation of others. If you need approval from others, you are also being held captive by the fear of them judging you. Free yourself from both extremes by abiding by your own inner compass. Be your own cheerleader. Internalize all the good others have ever given you and tap into it when you need to feel validated.

Nurture yourself. The most accomplished people are ones that have been encouraged along the way. If that is not your luck of the draw--to have someone cheering you on-- you must be your own best advocate. Think and say kind things about yourself.

Fight the compulsion or conditioning to diminish yourself. It does not make people like you more. It makes them feel less threatened by you. But healthy people gravitate to healthy friends. Be healthy in your relationship with yourself.

Your innate wisdom is always speaking to you through gut feelings. It is up to you to turn up the volume on that by actually paying attention. No one is going to bother with someone who doesn't listen to them, not even yourself. If you don't listen to your innate intelligence, it won't bother trying to be heard.

Encourage the individuality in others. It is the seedbed and invitation for a new crop of individuality. We awaken the genius in others when we allow them the space to express their uniqueness. Realize that seeing other people happy and fulfilled is a way of reflecting more happiness and fulfillment into the world.

16 HOW TO LIVE YOUR PURPOSE

- Dust off the things that brought you joy as a child.

- Take up old hobbies that you loved.

- Be spontaneous. When you feel like enjoying what makes you happy, don't allow excuses or time to get in the way. If you allot a certain time to do something, then "time", who is best friends with resistance, will talk you out of it. So do what you love when you feel like doing it and that will break through the resistance. Because resistance is being paralyzed in time and space.

- If you are restricted by a job, work what you love into the perimeters of your job as much as possible.

- Don't listen to others who say you have to choose a profession where you make a lot of money. Money can be a form of imprisonment if you are converting all your happiness into the illusion of the monetary system.

- Do what you love regardless of money. Musicians are the wealthiest people I know regardless of what's in their bank account.

- Being fixated on making money is like being fixated on the clock and only acknowledging twelve o'clock. There are so many more forms of abundance besides money and to only acknowledge monetary wealth is a form of selling your soul to linear existence.

- You don't need to know how to change the world in one sweeping decision. Move more and more in little steps to do things you love, and waste less and less energy in doing what you don't love.

- Get everybody else out of your head. Living your purpose is your sacred contract between you and the Universe. Other people's opinions or ideas for you are of no consequence and are only there to serve your resistance. This resistance makes doing what you love more glorious when you overcome it. Overcoming resistance is the flavor of life.

- Don't be afraid of letting people, places and things fall away on the way to living your purpose. A sculptor would have no success in creating their vision if they were afraid of chipping away pieces of stone.

- Don't share your dreams with anyone. This merely dissipates the energy and gives them the opportunity to diminish your passion in some way even if it is unintentional. Your purpose is your sacred journey. Don't outsource it to those who have strong opinions.

- Don't allow obstacles to limit you. Any pure intention fueled by a passion is invincible. The endurance of the human heart coupled by an encouraging mind have never been stretched to capacity.

- Whenever you get afraid you will fail, understand that love is the opposite of fear. So all you have to do is pour more love into your passion to dissipate any fear. In this way, use fear as a gauge for more love instead of something to react to.

- Know that the Universe supports you in manifesting your greatest accomplishments. Every inventor, innovator, creator and humanitarian who has ever achieved has been tested the way you are being tested in living your purpose. Take strength in realizing you are tapping into the fortitude of greatness in moving forward. Let this encourage you more.

- Give as you go. The act of empowering others allows you to advance as well. To wish the best for others is to tap into a source of empowerment that will sustain you more than the pettiness of coveting your own greatness. You will automatically be great in perpetuating the wellbeing of all.

17 HOW TO FINISH A PROJECT

Don't talk about it unless part of the project needs others involved. Then only talk about it to the people who are necessary to talk to WHEN it is necessary. Otherwise, you are bankrupting it of the energy that is needed to manifest it before it is able to generate energy of its own accord.

Work on it when the inspiration comes instead of allotting it to a specific time. The spontaneity attracts more energy to it.

Don't plan it out at the beginning, middle and end. This will stifle the fluidity. Allow for the creativity of change to blow in and shift it a little bit from the original vision, not enough to derail it, just enough so it can veer back into the rushing currents of productivity.

Stop yourself from doubting your abilities or capabilities to manifest the best version of the project as possible. Realize that when insecurities or doubts come up, they are merely being triggered to release. There is no invisible hand trying to squelch your success except your own.

Refrain from criticizing, judging or cursing the project or any aspect of the project in any way. These things are of a very heavy vibration. They can be like introducing a lead ball to a beautiful butterfly.

Don't compare the project to past attempts. This is you tapping into past engrams of when you have seemingly failed and adhering them to your new project. It is very limiting to compare one thing to another. Then you simply have two things that are forced to be the average of each other and are plucked from achieving their full potential.

Nail the project in coordinates of space and time as little as possible. This keeps the project "low to the ground" instead of allowing it to fly exponentially beyond time and space. That is where the creative currents blow.

Don't compare the project or yourself doing the project to anyone else. You want to keep in those exponential currents as much as possible.

Dream bigger than the project needs to be. You can even be tongue in cheek about it. If you want to make a million dollars, why not aim for a billion? Shoot beyond the stars to galaxies beyond this dimension.

Protect your project like a gestating baby because it is. Be as gentle and kind with your words and beliefs with your project as you would a newborn. Be as ruthless (in conviction) at defending it as a mama bear.

Break through resistance by forcing yourself to give the project attention even when you don't feel like it. This is working out deep issues for yourself. It is a primal experience to die while one is having a pretty good life. Sometimes, we play out this tragedy in future incarnations through not finishing projects and lamenting that they did not reach completion. It is best to just deal with our past deaths directly instead of using our energy to create half-finished projects in effigy of those lifetimes.

Don't try to please anyone else. It is impossible. People are not happy in their own skin. Don't give them the opportunity to project that onto you or your creations by caring what they think.

Infuse your uniqueness into the project. That is what is going to make it strike the consciousness of others more than trying to please their sense of aesthetics. Tapping into your unique way of looking at the world is a means of adding to the tapestry of humanity and expanding consciousness. Whatever you do differently than all others is your "four minute mile."

Be as bold and unabashed as possible in creating the perimeters of your project. You are the omniscient creator in this way. It is teaching everything that goes with such an empowering vantage point.

If you feel a project has run its course, don't just allow it to collect dust somewhere. Figure out a way to mark the project finished and send it out into the world. This will be a dynamic way of not allowing it to sit as a failure in your subconscious.

18 HOW TO GET YOUR MIRACLE

- Stop putting conditions on it.

- Stop thinking it has to come in a supernatural way.

- Put in an order for a miracle.

- Don't be jealous of other people's providence. Jealousy pinches the energy flow to the pipeline of abundance.

- Don't expect it to come through a certain person.

- Stop doubting.

- Stop micromanaging it.

- Quit waiting for the pot to boil. Take your attention off of expectations.

- Dream bigger than possible.

- Quit trying to figure out the pathway. They hardly ever come through expectations, only intentions.

- When you get evidence of miracles happening, show gratitude. Gratitude opens the pipeline to more blessings.

- Know you are worthy to receive.

- Get a sense that when you receive abundance, all others around you are uplifted as well.

- Stay positive. Positive energy is a conduit for miracles.

19 HOW TO TRANSCEND

Cut the Drama. The emotions are very low on the survival scale. Being reactionary is being in primal mode. So to be dramatic is to marry two low level vibrations. Existing in them is a means to ensure that you will stay at a primal level of existence. One cannot connect to truth and their deeper self if they are in reactionary mode. Even the crudest animals don't do this. Being dramatic is a very ignorant way to entertain yourself and ensure attention. It is pulling humanity down.

Refrain from all derogatory verbiage and behavior. This includes to yourself. The humility that has been ingrained in humanity is a form of having people inflict imprisonment on themselves. Humility is merely having the same sense of value for others as you do for yourself. There is no need to lower the bar on all of humanity by seeing yourself or others as low-lives. Those who control others do not do this. So all individuals need to take this "edge" away from power mongers by reseeding humanity. We do this when we see everyone with value and worth.

Speak clear truth. Insults are not truth. Truth has a neutral charge, not a negative one. Truth is not opinions or anything that is heard in the media. Truth comes from a depth that strikes the censors of the gut and heart. Listening to lies is not being polite. It is behaving untruthfully. If the neutrality of truth, real truth, hurts, then it is layers of illusion being ripped off of someone who identified with the illusion. These layers need to go from ourselves and all others. It doesn't mean it's our job to rip them off. It just means we shouldn't cringe from the task when we are led to speak truth by our higher self.

Stop defending a cause. All causes and ideologies are of the mind nature. There is a more expansive consciousness beyond them. Defending any cause or ideology is stating to the Universe and all others that you are afraid to transcend. Fear is the opposite of love.

Please stop defending God. God is the Source of all in its true essence. God does not need defending. God does not need the ego stroked. God has no ego. Man has been duped into worshiping a manmade concept. Anything that limits, diminishes, judges and impinges the freedom of individuals in any way is not mandated by God but the opposite. All of this worship of God in an unloving way towards others is following false prophets. ALL OF IT.

Delighting in debate, opinions and other mind games is only indulging and entertaining the ego. Nobody has learned truth by talking. Talking is a means of emanating your vibration out to others to proclaim you exist. It is fear based. The louder someone is, the more afraid they are in energy. Think about the people who are loudly playing their music in the car. At the core, they are not doing it to be irritating. They are doing it because they are terrified. In energy, they are doing it to keep predators away. It is easier to have compassion for them when you can realize this. In the same way, those who lecture others and tell them what to do are terrified in energy of how little they know.

Stop competing with others. Stop one-upping others. This means there is no hierarchy, comparisons, or trying to emulate others. Everyone is a starburst. Their uniqueness is in their unpredictable emanations. This is their display against the backdrop of conformity. If you try to align two starbursts, you hinder both of their patterns of emanation. You drop them both out of the sky.

Root for the other gal. Life isn't about bettering others. Life is about all of us being the best. This is how we raise the bar on humanity. Those inspiring images of one runner carrying the other runner over the finish line is a great analogy of how to live. Let's carry each other over the finish line in all the ways that we can. Allowing ourselves to be carried over the finish line when relevant is important too. Practicing random kindness is the mainstay in a loving existence. That is why being kind feels so good; it is contributing to raising the bar on humanity.

Stop converting all forms of abundance to the monetary system. It is old currency. Doing something that you don't love does not make you happy, taxes your body or makes you unhappy, and is a form of selling your soul for money. Your energy system runs and thrives on joy, truth and love. If you do not love what you do, and it does not bring you joy, then you are not being truthful to yourself. An energy system that does what it loves perpetually feeds itself. One that doesn't may have monetary wealth but taxes humanity in a different way. The rich think those who don't generate great wealth are a tax on society. But those who live only to generate more wealth at the cost of a clean and safe environment are taxing all of humanity.

Bring creativity, imagination, individual expression and enthusiasm back to life. These were all but stripped out of humanity by the power mongers who tried to enslave us all to a linear existence. But they were not merely attempting to enslave us on earth; they were attempting to dry up our afterlife as well. Our afterlife consists of the God stuff we generate in this life. A renaissance of creativity and expression is needed not only to generate goodness on earth but also to reseed the heavens. This is the great necessity of having children: to regenerate the imagination of us all. Programming them extra early with stringent schedules and computers is robbing all of humanity of their childlike wonder as a resource to regenerate our own creative expression.

This is a short list. If people can digest some of these truths and emanate them out into humanity as a mainstay, we will be well on our way to getting back on course to worldwide peace.

20 THE WONDER OF LIFE

People aren't nasty because they don't care. They may care too much and push people away because they can't handle any more hurt.

People who are overly nice are not better people than everyone else. They have merely figured out a way to protect themselves from being attacked.

People who are agreeable don't necessarily agree. They may have stuffed their truth down so far out of fear of being called out for it that they will say anything to continue the deception.

People who disagree are not sworn enemies. They merely have a different dictionary of experiences and references than we do. We were all congealed together at the core with the same love force.

People who always give may not be more generous than others. They may use giving as a means of having a superiority over others. They may be too selfish to receive and allow others to experience that same advantage.

People who take are not necessarily selfish. They may be stuck in the primal belief that the Universe will not offer them anything freely. They use taking as a lifeboat to feel safety in the enormity of existing.

People who lie may simply not know themselves. They believe in their omniscience enough to manifest in word what they desire to manifest in deed.

People who tell the truth are fearless and loving. No matter how stark the truth is, it takes courage to gift truth to others without dressing it up in fancy or fiction.

People who Love are awakened. They see wonder in all life and dissipate all the corners of doubt with the bright beacon of their convictions.

People who fail are reliving old memories of not measuring up. They are not incompetent but may merely be repeating an old pattern that seems comfortable.

People who succeed do so in increments of a thousand tiny failures and discouragements. It is only the conviction at an incredibly deep level that overrides all inclinations to give up.

People who assist others know their own essence. They see their beauty and failings in the faces of all of life. They are kind to strangers because it is showing a kindness to an aspect of themselves that has been judged and diminished. When we love others, we are embracing our true nature and seeing the synergy, empowerment and wonder of life.

21 WAYS TO OPEN UP YOUR ENERGY FIELD

- Find ways to speak your truth.
- Compromise.
- Be around people who honor you.
- Do what you love.
- Listen to your instincts and gut feelings.
- Immerse yourself in the beauty of your world and find ways to bring that to others.
- Stay immersed in the present.
- Lather praise upon yourself shamelessly.
- Be accepting of all and still bless them with your best intention.
- Be loving and kind.
- Ignore all the evidence of negativity in the world and focus on the beauty here: Trees, nature, beautiful water.
- Feel empowered by using visualization techniques to turn every negative scenario into a positive reality.
- Develop a God complex and encourage this in all others to breed individual empowerment.
- Always be truthful.

- Put out positive intentions and follow through with them as much as you are capable.

- Practice the Spiritual Law of Silence.

- Spend time in nature.

- Be around loving people who appreciate you.

- Be happy with your own company.

- Follow your own instincts.

- Have only kind intentions towards anyone.

- See jealousy as a gauge to where to work on yourself and nothing more.

- Remove all time restrictions on yourself.

- Engage in hobbies and doing what you love.

- Realize everyone is doing their best and take nothing that they do personally.

- Concentrate on your own state of affairs with no judgment to others. Never feel compelled to compare yourself to anyone. This is merely pulling back the reins on one of you.

- Realize that current affairs are showing us the most negative things life offers. Realize how validating that the majority can see these now. Realize that these negative actions have always transpired and now they are flushed out. See the upgrade in this.

- Bow out of outmoded belief systems, dogma and practices that tire you out and don't have a positive outcome, like holidays.

- Question beliefs that no longer serve you.

- Realize that the world is ever changing and we create the world we live in with our thoughts and intentions. So empower yourselves to make it a positive world.

- Relax and trust that innate goodness will prevail.

- Shift your focus from thinking to knowing. Anything that you need an answer to will be fed into you when you need it through the process of direct knowing. This happens when you are immersed in the moment. Thinking takes you out of the moment.

- Forgo all drama and see it as the attention getting device that it is. Validate people when they are positive and calm, not when they are milking you for attention.

- Knowing your worth as an omniscient, omnipresent, omnipotent atom of God.

- Bow out of all competition. Use your energy to maintain your own level of calm and resolve.

- Bow out of the linear world that has you behaving like a stick figure and know yourself as the exponential starburst that you really are.

- Be grateful…It is the quickest way.

22 HOW TO CONNECT WITH YOUR SPIRIT GUIDES

Don't worry about figuring out who your Guides are. There are so many Guides and helpers on the other side that trying to figure out who they are is like thinking you may know someone because you know someone with the same last name.

Guides are mentors. They are not interested in being worshiped. Worshiping them or adulating them is a way of keeping them at bay because you keep yourself at a lower vantage point. It is never helpful to anyone to put anyone on a pedestal. Think of your Guides as more like best friends than someone to adulate. Keep the respect. Just lose the adoration. They will still be larger than life. But with a tweak in this dynamic, you can expand your consciousness to be present with them. They are always present with you. It is you that has to shift from the human consciousness to be present with them.

Have conversations with them in your mind. If you get information, that may be their guidance. Don't ask a third party for validation. Learning to listen and communicate with your Guides is a form of turning up the volume on your own awareness. It is part of the process of awakening. Asking a third party is a form of giving your power away and is counter to the empowerment needed to connect to your Guides.

Don't be afraid of what others may think of you. The Ancient Ones are immersed in Love. Even being self-conscious is a form of fear. Fear is the opposite of Love. Whenever you are diminishing yourself with self-consciousness, you have to let it go to be more conscious. It is a form of a paradox.

Pay attention to subtle cues that are spiritual lessons throughout your day. Everything that is happening around us is a cue to our spiritual lessons. The more we look for the lessons, the more we will see the synchronicity during our day.

When you awake, put out the intention like an invitation for your Guides to make their presence known to you. They are ever present. It is you that must hone your awareness to be able to perceive them. Imagine them watching you as you go through your day. This may help dry up any residual negative behavior or language. Just being able to remind yourself of their presence during the day is a discipline. It is stretching the capacity or your awareness.

Be loving and kind at all times. If not merely to be loving and kind, your actions raise your vibrations. Anything you can do to raise your vibrations also raises your consciousness. Since the Ancient Ones are immersed in Love, the more loving you are, the closer you are to their vibration.

Pay attention to what people say and all the other messages you hear during the day. These are messages from your Guides. If you notice a continuing theme when you talk to different people or have different experiences, take heed. These are your Guides speaking through all life.

Pay attention to unexpected visitors. Animals, nature and strange occurrences are used to get a point across to someone who is still afraid of being approached by their Guides.

Think and say only positive things. It is a quick way of raising your vibratory rate to be at the closer frequency to your Guides. Stop the self-derision. If you don't believe you are worthy, your Guides won't waste their energy fighting the human resistance.

Mock up walking and talking with your Guides through the day. You can actually feel their protection from negativity the more you do this.

Remember your connection with your imagination, nature, your toys and other childlike musings. Children are naturally able to tap into their awakened self. Perhaps you have had conversations with your Guides when you were very young and merely forgot. Perhaps remembering your childhood and re-entering that innocent state is a shortcut to connecting to your Guides.

Set the intention to visit with your Guides during the dream state. The dream censor garbles truth so as not to overload the conscious mind. So when you have dreams of someone you respect, it is most likely your Guides taking a form that is positive to you. Pay attention to the positive people that appear in your dreams. The positive traits they display are the special traits of your Guides.

Pay attention to your dreams. These are nuggets of truth for you to discern. Pay attention to your dream symbols during the day. The more attention you put on discerning truth, the more you will train yourself to perceive truth. It is you striving for more connection in a comfortable way that will assist you in connecting with your Guides. It is not a desperate climb up a steep mountain. It is a leisurely hike up a spiraling hill.

Keep what is sacred to you to yourself. It is really easy for others to burst our bubble of enthusiasm. This is true with all that we hold sacred as well. It may not even be safe to share with a spouse. It is not that they can't be trusted. It is that you are trying to pull the sublime into a linear world. Take inventory of your reasons to share. Do you want to appear special, need approval, or are you trying to recruit your spouse to your level of awareness? None of these reasons will fly with a Guide. They have been with us longer than one life. They care less about the backdrop of our activities here. To them it is like a teacher obsessing over the lesson on the chalkboard. This life is just a prop for you to hone your spiritual awareness.

Listen more, talk less. Every aspect of our day is a teacher. It is up to us to respect the classroom. If we go on autopilot, it is turning down the volume of our awareness. It is our choice not to listen to truth.

Pay attention to your gut and heart feelings. These are energy sensors for perceiving truth, as valid as your eyes and ears are as sensory receptors.

Validate all others as you go. Your Guides not only care about what is precious to you, but they are actually teaching you to be a Guide also. This is how humanity perpetuates truth and understanding. So realize it is not about you. It is about how you can help others. This is a means of preventing the awareness that you glean from becoming a stagnant state. Truth, love, kindness and awareness must keep moving and flowing to stay pure.

23 CONNECT WITH YOUR GUIDES

(Say each statement three times while tapping on your head and say it a fourth time while tapping on your chest.)

"I release putting my Guides on a pedestal; in all moments."

"I release treating knowing my Guides as an unattainable goal; in all moments."

"I walk joyfully and unabashedly with my Guides; in all moments."

"I am equal to my Guides; in all moments."

"I am centered and empowered in friendship with my Guides; in all moments."

"I resonate, emanate and am interconnected with my Guides in divine love; in all moments."

24 UPGRADES IN SPIRITUAL BELIEF SYSTEM IN THE FIFTH DIMENSION

There is no concern over taking on karma. This is a subtle form of fear and fear is the antithesis of healing. One needs to just make their love bigger to dissipate any fear that they are experiencing. In the fifth dimension, we realize we are not trapped in a linear existence. This means we are not limited to being a physical body. We can make our energy as big as a galaxy so there is no limited body to hold someone else's karma in.

There is no longer relying on the belief that "all is as it should be." In the fifth dimension, there is an understanding of our own empowerment and any issue can be addressed in such a dynamic way. Saying, "all is as it should be," is a very subtle form of feeling powerless and creates an apathetic state in some cases.

There is no need for Akashic records. We no longer need to relive mistakes and tragedies we have experienced in a past life. We have a clean slate. It is like graduating from grade school and no longer needing crayons and scissors.

People no longer withhold healing others because they didn't give consent. This is as silly as not assisting an abused dog that is tied up to a post. They may not consent to being helped, but it is obvious that they don't realize that they need help. In energy, everyone is asking for help. That is what prayers are.

No longer do people expect to be saved by a faceless God. They realize that we are all the face of God and when we pray for help, help will come through other people. We also realize that we are all the face of God so we honor all beings as sacred. This is how we pay homage to God. Hypocrisy in worship is eliminated in where we pay homage to God and then turn around and judge and diminish others. We can't possibly honor God and diminish others.

Labels will no longer be necessary. We are all psychics, mediums, and healers. We are all connected. We are one big self. No longer is there separating ourselves using labels. If I am a healer, you are a healer. We are a compilation of us all.

If someone is suffering in the microcosm, it is a reflection of the ills of the macrocosm. To heal the planet, you address the symptoms in individuals. Apathy is no longer an option.

Individuals are no longer left to sink or swim for themselves. The belief system that one's personal issues are necessary to spiritually strengthen them is obsolete. This would be true if the deck wasn't so stacked against the individual by power mongers and the greedy. Your helping someone else may be the spiritual test for you to overcome residual hesitancy to get involved. The way we overcome the limitations of the third dimension is to change the setting on our energy system from taking to giving. Once we become habitual givers, there is a self-sustaining mechanism implemented that immerses us in the perpetual state of being.

We are no longer trapped in linear existence. Time is not linear and neither is existence. A minute spent in doing what we love is different than a minute doing what we hate. If we stay in the perpetual state of being in the moment, we drop out of the limiting state of time and space. If we find ourselves "juggling", it is indicative that we are in linear instead of exponential being. In exponential being, we merely stand in our center and allow all issues to rotate to our attention and address them then instead of juggling.

Earth is no longer seen as a hopeless war based planet. That belief in itself is an apathetic state. Earth is the heart chakra of the lower worlds. It is dire that earth is empowered in a loving state of free will. This opens the capabilities of all the lower worlds. All limiting states instated by power mongers is released.

Creativity, imagination and enthusiasm are the lifeblood of the fifth dimension. People don't realize that the creativity they exude expands consciousness. This includes heaven. The belief that heaven will be there waiting for someone is as silly as believing they are due an inheritance they didn't contribute to. When we cross over, it is a reflection of the creativity and imagination we have put into this life. It is important to strive to be empowered and original to expand our consciousness when we cross over. Those who are visionaries are creating a more expansive reality in the non-physical world for everyone. You are welcome.

Dreams are a reflection of our life outside of the physical skin. They are not just random symbols, but our higher self trying to instill in our physical self, higher truths. They are worth taking the time to study.

We no longer work to achieve perfection. Perfection is an illusion that prevents people from embracing their uniqueness. There is freedom in individuality. This is us embracing our exponential empowerment. We no longer perceive ourselves as stick figures in a linear world but realize that we are starbursts eager to realize our own potential.

There is no need to spend hours trying to get out of the body. Our empowerment is engaged in being fully grounded and engaged in our physical existence and expanding our consciousness to encompass all of the Universe while being aware in the physical realms as well.

All groups are outmoded as people take back their individuality and stop giving their effectiveness away to drive the engines of power.

Nature and trees are appreciated as more important than monetary currency. Trees are seen as the wise sentient beings they are. They are given respect and sovereignty as individuals and wise counsel.

Humans no longer consider themselves superior to other beings. They realize their true edge is to be able to convert the dynamic energy into creative force which is the atmosphere of higher consciousness. They realize that reasoning is the building block of this ability.

Communication with other beings will be commonplace as people learn to perceive in energy rather than rely on the clumsy guttural sounds of words. By perceiving in energy, all will perceive truth and lies. This inability to get away with lies will bring accountability and integrity back to the world.

These things are all in place, but people have brought their illusion of the third dimension into the fifth dimension as a form of comfort while they adjust. That is why healing is so possible now. Everyone is already whole and healed. It is more a matter of dropping old engrams that say otherwise.

Female energy is empowered so that humans can regain their sensitivities. Compassion, ingenuity, and benevolence are all yin-based attributes. As female energy regains a footing in consciousness, so will the attributes that it represents.

25 STAY CLOSED TO PSYCHIC INTRUSION

Don't answer questions about yourself from people who don't need to know the answer. They may be merely fishing for their own advantage in reference to you.

Don't seek permission from people who are not in authority. It is a way of giving your power away.

Don't ask advice from anyone who is not in a position to know the answer.

Don't interject yourself in conversations that are not concerning you.

Don't give advice that no one has asked for.

When you are in public places and your mood changes suddenly, try to equivocate it with your surroundings. For instance, if you are in the mall and start feeling desperate about finances, it could be you are walking into the energy of someone who was there before you. Just like you can stand in someone's pee in a pool, you can stand in someone's sadness in the mall. Try to shake feelings off so as not to keep the ones that aren't yours.

Understand the energy exchange behind everything that transpires. Much of language is meant to subjugate each other. Comparisons are a way to level your individuality. Saying "Don't do that or that will happen," is a curse we put on each other. Many of people's opinions are a curse so don't open yourself up to them.

Asking someone's opinion many times is seeking validation. Know that you don't need to be validated by anyone else.

If you accept a gift from someone, you are allowing their energy into your own field. It is best not to accept gifts from someone you don't like.

If you have an aversion to someone, something or some place, pay attention to it. Your innate intelligence is telling you something. If you get a bad feeling going somewhere, it may be because it is not healthy for you energetically.

You know when you are not being respected. Don't go or be anywhere where you are not honored. Obligation is no excuse. You are too important.

Respect the rights of others. There is no quicker way for the Universe to give you lessons on your blind spots than to put you in the position of those you have judged. Pay attention to whom you judge and see if you do not see the grain of similarity in your own experiences.

Refuse to take sides when two loved ones are in disagreement. When two people in your circle have an argument, you may be recruited as the moral compass. Refrain from allowing your ego to be stroked in this way.

26 REASONS PEOPLE ARE NOT FREE

- They think too much.
- They worry about what other people think.
- They get caught up in drama.
- They focus on other people's lives more than their own.
- They allow the outside world to dictate their narrative.
- They confuse concepts like humility with unworthiness.
- They worry too much about what they look like.
- They worry too much about making money.
- They don't trust their relationship with the Universe.
- They subscribe to a pecking order of life and don't see themselves at the top of it.
- They have cut off their connection with their own depth through not delving into their past lives.
- They believe anything they are told as truth.
- They believe truth can actually exist in the form and function of life.

- They dilute their energy by saying things they don't mean.

- They dilute their energy by making promises they don't keep.

- They secretly know they are special and hide this knowledge from the masses.

- They have been compared to others into conformity.

- They lost the ability to perceive in energy.

- They frame many of the blessings they receive as curses.

- They accrue things to feel safe.

- They are afraid to be separate from their consciousness.

- They are limited by a male slanted point of view.

- They have given their power away.

- They don't realize that their power is energy and they can take it back.

- They stopped believing in fairies.

- They stopped holding space for good things to happen.

- They have stopped pouring their energy into the God realms that are formed through their efforts.

- They stopped believing in God so they stopped believing in heaven or any form of life except what they are used to.

- They have been pitted against each other lifetime after lifetime.

- They stopped formulating creative intentions that manifest the wonder in life.

- They dream small.

- They stopped dreaming.

- They stopped playing.

- They stopped hoping.

- They stopped knowing.

- They stopped loving.

- They stopped giving.

- They stopped being.

27 I STAND BY MY CONVICTIONS

Speak kindness where it has never been spoken.

Allow others to form their own opinions.

Preach ONLY to the choir.

See greatness where it stands.

Respect all souls in all forms.

Suspend all judgment.

Bow out of all disagreement.

See the world as a wonderful, beautiful place.

28 I AM NOT ALONE TODAY

There is no one in my life who wishes to spend time with me today. No one really cares about me. I don't matter. I must be so annoying to be around that no one wants to even extend human kindness to me. It is irrelevant to everyone here whether I exist or not. I must be hard to Love. I don't even attract life partners because there is nothing attractive about me.

These are the thoughts that the human consciousness of the mind bombard me with. These are the thoughts that induce pain and dredge up old instances of injury and indignation. But I choose to turn down the channel on such silly notions. I listen to my heart.

This is what the heart tells me:

Being with people is a distraction. The Universe is strengthening your capacity to be imbued with love by not having you believe that it originates from other people.

You give so much of yourself. You need to pour that love into the world and not waste it on those who feel entitled to it.

You are being blessed to have all the humans pushed out of your life so that you can develop your ability to love other species of life and have an intimate relationship with life itself.

You are too aware to be trapped in the conventions of social culture. If the Universe left it to you, you would be distracted all the days of your life trying to please and placate others.

Everything that you are given daily in life lessons and spiritual awareness becomes a part of you even when you cross over. You are rich and abundant beyond compare in the spiritual realms. Others are starving for your spiritual gifts. Don't waste energy or momentum by focusing on those around you who don't see your greatness.

Isn't life a thorough teacher to provide you with a buffer from people adoring you? All those around you who don't see your greatness assist you so well in staying focused on the sanctity of the moment and not being distracted by the illusions.

No one can see you because so few people see truth, beauty and love in the world. You resonate so closely to truth, beauty and love that you have indeed become invisible to the average human.

Your Spiritual light is very bright. For some humans, it blinds them. In this world of illusion, the way they respond to that is by being put off by you. But that is only more reason to have compassion for them.

All the security and material comfort that humans strive to accrue is only their limited attempt to own the intangible gifts that come so readily to you.

The Universe is gifting you with isolation to help you drop out of the illusion of the moment and become alive, aware and expansive in the true interconnection of all.

God is not punishing you. You are being gifted with great insight and lasting spiritual capabilities every moment. By ignoring the mind's taunting, you are awakening to the sanctity of all life.

You and your gifts are so important to the world that you are not allowed to waste this existence being caught up in the illusion of the day and the pettiness of man.

Thanksgiving is a day to teach others as a group how to be grateful and how to interconnect with others. You have already learned these lessons so you do not need to go through the tedious lesson plans that other humans need.

Wanting what other humans have is like wishing to go back to kindergarten because you like coloring. You create masterpieces, my friend. Use your abilities to do so.

These are some of the things that my heart tells me. It also tells me that I am being used as an example to show people how the shift from human consciousness to spiritual consciousness is done. It also tells me that there are those out there who need to hear this. That this is what their hearts have been telling them as well. Those who need to hear this will find this message and realize that they are loved and important in the scheme of life. They matter and are more dear than all the homespun celebrations can convey.

Please get a sense of how important you are to life and the transcendence process from the mundane to the dynamic. Use any pain that you may endure as a benchmark of the greatness of your true self. May you realize your true worth in the expansion of consciousness. You matter. You really do. You are loved beyond compare. You really are.

Some will argue with this that they can't matter because they don't outshine others in this life. You are not paying attention. It is a lie of the human consciousness that you must be great on the backs of others. That is how male energy has programmed the world.

But female energy embraces greatness as a sisterhood where all are happiest when everyone is at their best. That is the reality of where human awareness is headed. By dropping out of the lies of the illusion, you can plug into the expansiveness of the ultimate truth. As one succeeds in the true sense, we all succeed.

Here is to the success of the human species to transcend. I love you all. Every single one of you. Because I can. And that is a gift that human loneliness has afforded me. I would not trade that for anything.

29 YOU KNOW THAT EXCRUCIATING LONELINESS?

You know that excruciating loneliness that we deal with? It is not to punish. It is to awaken us from the arrogance that human eyes are the only ones that can see us. That human ears are the only ones that listen. That the warmth of another person is the only comfort afforded.

When we are so disappointed by the lack of appreciation in fellow humans, we can drop out of our lack of appreciation for all other beings. It is then that we can, hold all life in reverence and friendship. It is then, and only then, we can realize that we are never really alone.

30 HOW TO USE SPEECH TO EMPOWER YOURSELF

Everything we say is a command for the 3D printer that is our great mind. Think of it in those absolute terms. You can't expect your computer to discern when you are joking and when you are serious. So don't expect that from your mind. If you hit the send button, you know a document is sent. In the same way, when you utter statements, no matter how tongue in cheek they are to you, you are launching them into the Universe to manifest.

Our words are our latitude and longitude of where we are in life. Words like hope, need, want or faith put us at a disadvantaged reference point. It positions us away from the desired results. It is better to know, have, trust and be.

Hope is a position of weakness. It leaves you at the mercy of intangible variables. It is more empowering to know than to hope. Knowing sits you right smack dab in the middle of an experience. When you know, you know. When you hope, you are waiting in the dark.

Faith is also positioned away from the desired results. If you have faith, you are passively waiting for something to reveal itself to you. When you trust, it is a position of confidence. When you trust, you are aligned with the latitude and longitude of the desired results.

Watch your colloquialisms. They are designed to put limitations on you. For example, when something good happens to you and you say, "I can't believe it," what you really are saying is that it is unfathomable that something good happened to you. When you are saying your heart is broken, what you are telling yourself is that the vessel that works non-stop from the moment of your birth to keep you alive is fragile. You are saying YOU are fragile. When you say the expression, "whatever," you are telling the Universe to send you any experience in the mix because you are apathetic and indifferent to life.

When you use curse words, you are really cursing yourself. You are using a coarse vibration to ensure that you STAY in a pattern of coarse vibration. You are preventing yourself from getting closer to truth, love and even self-awareness because curse words vibrate at a much different frequency than higher consciousness.

Words are vibrations of what you attract. They are the latitudes and longitudes to where you position yourself in life. When you talk about disease, problems and complaints, you are positioning yourself to accept more of these graciously as a welcomed friend.

When you say the name of diseases, you are making it easier for your body to accept these diseases into itself. That is why awareness for negative things is not helpful but actually TOXIC. It is ignorance that drives people to campaign for awareness for certain diseases. All it does is put a welcome mat on our lives for these issues to be prevalent in our lives. It is much better to honor the health of individuals, along with their strength and resilience, than to brand them as survivors of any disease.

We are all survivors. The ones who do not attract experiences into them are the ones to emulate. They are not ones who need a negative depiction of themselves to wear as a badge of honor. This sounds insensitive because psychic energies that advocate for disease have conditioned us to create heroes out of victims. This is merely to keep us enslaved to disease.

At a certain point, the mind loses sight that it is honoring the victims of the disease and just ends up honoring the disease. This is what these campaigns for certain issues are actually doing. Because the vibration of the words cancer and diabetes don't change if we are fighting them or honoring their victims. Both are marrying the vibration of the word into our state of being. It would be beneficial for people to understand this.

Replace all passive words with positive self-proclaiming words. Don't say, "If I win a million dollars." Say, "When I win a million dollars." If you are not going to state it to the Universe for all to hear, how are you going to accept it into your life as a reality for all to see?

Please stop owning negative issues. Saying "my" anything nails it to your energy field and labels it as part of the experience of being you. People are so proud of owning a negative diagnosis because it gives them a little attention in the form of sympathy. But this is very short lived. People then have to live with the label when the crowds die down and it's the dark of night. Some people try to amp up this attention by adding more and more issues onto them for sympathy. After a while, the burden of knowing that person becomes too heavy. Their negative vibration is palpable. Friends fall away for self-survival. It is best to just address each issue we encounter as an experience that is passing through, NOT something that now defines us or that we own.

Some people accept an issue if it is prevalent in their family lineage. It is not so much that this issue is handed down through their genetic make-up. It is more that having the issue gives the person an intimate connection with a family member if they share a disease. Someone who lost their parent to a certain diagnosis may willingly accept a similar diagnosis as inevitable because it makes them feel more special to share it with their loved one.

31 THE QUICKEST ROUTE TO TRANSCENDENCE

Water takes different forms. So does consciousness. In a way, they are similar. In water, there is solid (ice), liquid and gas (air).

It is really important for water to stay fluid to maintain its purity. If it sits too long, it becomes stagnant and must be dumped into the ground to be purified through passing through the soil and recollecting itself into a running stream.

All of this is similar to the human consciousness. Some individual molecules of human consciousness are very rigid in their belief system. They live a fear-based life. They are like ice. Most are a mixture of fear and love so they function well enough but still have their limitations. They are in the "water" stage.

Some people are looking around and realizing all the limitations that have been put on them. They are starting to discern truth for themselves. They are looking around and questioning all the conditioning that has been put on us and realize that they have not really been born into a truthful reality. These people have started the evaporation process.

The evaporation process is when water moves from liquid to gas. In the human consciousness, the evaporation process is referred to as awakening, enlightenment or transcendence. We, as a species, are in the process of evaporating. We will still have the same properties of "water." We will still have awareness of ourselves and all the positive aspects of being "water." We will just have more spaciousness to live, breath, think, emote, love and be joyful than ever before.

When all of humanity is in this state, we will have transcended together. It is a scary process for many because they have an understanding of life based on the lies believed by "ice" people. One cannot be ice and air at the same time. Individual atoms may evaporate which is what happens when we drop the physical form. But for the whole state of the world to change, all the properties of ice must be dissipated.

Anger, manipulation, greed, bigotry, and selfishness are all aspects of the ice people. The bond that holds the ice molecules together in society is fear. It is glue, a very strong bonding glue. Some people enjoy being ice. They enjoy the power and security of it. There is fear in being water and that fear keeps them in ice form.

They love being ice so much that they administer fear to others merely to have company in the ice state. Ice isn't ice unless there is more than one molecule of it. It takes a lot of fear these days to keep people bonding in ice. It is a hard state to keep forcing onto others. So those who love ice and are good at it have introduced lies to everyone.

They tell them they must behave a certain way, believe a certain thing or worship a certain way, or there will be negative consequences. They know that fear is a way to keep people in ice consciousness. Instead of always needing to work to keep them in a state of fear, they introduce these beliefs that will cause the individuals to keep themselves in a state of fear. It is effortless. They up the stakes on all the individuals and make them fearful of others. That way they will work to keep not only themselves in a state of fear, they will keep their neighboring molecules glued in fear as well.

These ice-loving individuals figured out that love made people more fluid. They knew love dissipated the fear. So they had to really trick people into staying ice. So they took the purest concept they could imagine, which was the creator of all, and gave it qualities to induce fear. Since the real Source was loving and kind, they could not allow people to gravitate to it because that would transform them into water and perhaps even help them evaporate consciously into air.

So they conditioned all individuals through painful indoctrination to see the benevolent creator as a ruthless overlord, someone who inflicted pain and punishment. They called him God. Man did ruthless, horrible things to others and said it was the will of God. These people so wanted to stay in the ice consciousness that they created the total opposite attributes of Source and had man worship the opposite of Source. This would ensure that they never would transcend.

Another thing they did to immerse individuals in fear was to introduce the concept of death. They confused the beautiful experience of evaporation or transcendence with something that they conjured as horrific and final. They made people believe that the temporary shift in consciousness of one lifetime was the finality of it all. They halted their understanding of themselves experiencing many lifetimes of evaporating and becoming condensation again and again.

They instilled this belief system as an outer mandate. If someone felt the innate sense of truth, wonder and expression within themselves, the other individuals would turn on them. They would demonize and stigmatize them. They were burned at the stake as witches, shunned from society, labeled tree huggers, hippies, flakes, all the while preventing the truth, love and expansiveness of consciousness that these individuals were experiencing from melting the ice. This torturing of advanced souls became so systemic that the mere thought of transcending induced individuals into fear. This was a perfect way to keep everyone as ice.

The problem for those who love the security of being ice is that there are too many individuals veering towards transcending. It is not enough to demonize individuals anymore. To stay as ice, there needs to be a mass agreement that these individuals are evil. The ice lovers must introduce even more fear to the mix to prevent them from transcending. So they make an enemy out of all those who are gearing towards transcendence.

They give them a label to be able to identify them clearly. They call them left wings. They deem them the enemy. They could be our children, parents or friends. But they still become the enemy that is trying to destroy us. When in actuality, the love that we all experience is the conduit that keeps us all connected as water. They are not our enemy. They are an aspect of ourselves. They are us in another form with a different set of conditions that affords them a different vantage point. We are all one component.

When water does not flow though, it becomes stagnant. If the ice lovers can't keep us all in the consciousness of ice, they will do the next best thing. They will have us turn on ourselves as enemies and prevent our fluid movement within ourselves. This is what we are seeing with trying to prevent individuals from migrating around the world. The walls we build enforce a stagnant state of consciousness. Creating a stagnant state of consciousness is the next best thing to being ice for those who prefer to be ice. They strive to keep us immersed in a state of apathy.

A way to prevent this is for those who are love based to continue to be love based. The ice lovers WANT everyone to turn away from love and stay immersed in fighting. That is considered a win for them. They will do everything they can to keep humanity immersed in negativity and fear at all costs. That is the only way they prevent the natural evolution of transcendence which is happening.

If they can turn peace lovers back into fear mongers, then they have been effective. That is why raising awareness on horrific issues can be counterproductive. If we all raise our awareness onto love, peace and truth, we will be more effective than taking on an individual plight. Many times, those who do this are doing the work of those who want to stay ice.

To counter this, if you are love based, continue to be love based. If there are those who limit themselves and others, have compassion for them because you were once at that phase too. Encourage them with loving intentions. You were once the most despicable you could be as well. It is a fantastic way to learn power. You abused power once. Now you suffer with those memories. This drives the need to do anything you can not to ever abuse power again.

Let the Trumps of the world learn their lessons quickly and thoroughly. Have compassion for the anguish they inflict on themselves. Dissipate their fear with your love. Encourage them inwardly that they will be fine and that all fear is a temporary state. They are praying for guidance from a vengeful man made God. May they be answered by a truthful, loving expression of Source. Be the molecule of God that answers them. It is the quickest, most efficient route to transcendence.

32 WHAT AWARE SOULS DO

Energy matches the vibration of the things it clings to just like dew clings to a morning leaf. That dew could believe it is a part of the leaf. That is what it "knows" as its identity. In the same way, the energies that collect within an area can take on personal characteristics.

A house is full of all your thoughts, emotions and habitual interactions bouncing around and permeating the atmosphere. There is no need to sensationalize it or give it further life by being fearful of it. It is merely a condensation and collection of human interactions, identifying with those actions and thus it develops a persona.

Fear and inactivity are great ways to coagulate the energy. Inactivity slows down the natural flow of energy. Just as pure water will stagnate if it is left standing still, so will energy. Most issues in the body will clear up if you simply remove the fear and move fresh energy into it. This is why people with open minds and open hearts, in general, are more healthy. Their energy, as it is implied by the word "open," is more fluid so they do not collect stagnancy in the body as easily.

Complaining, gossiping, judging, and labeling are all ways of coagulating the energy. Regret stops the movement of energy cold. Kindness, acceptance, the non-reactionary state and gratitude are means of keeping the energy flowing. Put an open minded person next to a bigoted one and you can see the difference in how stagnant energy pinches the features and the intellect of the bigot. The open-minded person's features and energy will remain more round and open. Stagnant energy ages a person.

Western medicine is big on labeling issues. This is a means of coagulating the energy further so it has actual mass and weight. When an issue has mass and weight, it is a validation for western medicine. Western medicine is based on these validations. Of course, your mind being a 3D printer can produce anything you program it to, even disease.

Alternative medicine deals more obliquely with issues. Energy workers see the issue for what it is: blocked and stagnant energy. They don't use the blockage as validation for their work; they use the absence of blockages to validate it. That is why people who are more immersed in materialism gravitate to western medicine. People who don't need such validation remain healthier.

Many people need their results to be concrete evidence because they have lost the ability to perceive in energy. They are flying blind in this way and cling to the most validating means of reacting. Unfortunately, this includes burning or cutting away at their beautiful body at the site of the clogged energy instead of merely figuring out what is causing the blockage and releasing it.

Alternative medicine is an oxymoron because it is the one most natural and conducive to wellness. Our body deals with releasing stagnant energy on a regular basis. It is a natural process that happens literally as naturally as breathing. As you inhale, your body breath is scanning the body for blockages. As you exhale it is releasing and repairing them.

Our body deals with these blockages on a regular basis. If left alone, the body will remove these blockages naturally before a person has an inclination to put a label on them. But once a diagnosis is involved, the conscious mind gets involved with fear, dread, and mocking up worst case scenarios. Once this happens, it coagulates the issue even more so and is more difficult to remove. This is why western medicine preaches early detection. Its validation depends on the conscious mind getting involved and coagulating the energy further to create a more solid diagnosis.

When the body gets overwhelmed with issues, it will store them in the diaphragm to release later when the body is in a more relaxed state. If it can't get to them in due time, it will bubble wrap them in a fat cell and store them in the body to release later.

That is why losing weight is so difficult for some. It isn't merely about decreasing the intake of food. It is about creating a more fluid atmosphere for energy to move around the body while unpacking all the emotional issues it has packed in fat cells. When losing weight, you are dealing with all the emotional issues that were once stored. You are unpacking them to release. That is why people are so moody when dieting. But if they become more active, it is a way of processing these issues more readily.

Being healthy in general entails keeping your energy as fluid as possible. If you think about the past too much, it creates a stoppage of your emotional energy. If you worry about the future too much it creates a stoppage of your mental energy. If you are too sedentary, it causes you to regret the moment and revert to either the past or present too easily. Physical, emotional and mental energy are all important to keep fluid.

That is another reason personal beliefs need to change as well as physical and emotional points to be optimally healthy. Beliefs cause a collecting point for stagnant energy in the body. Everything else in the body could be moving at a great pace. But these beliefs that may be so ingrained may be markers in our energy system that can cause a literal sticking point in our health.

Things like religious limitations, genetic markers and emotional attachments to ethnicity or opinions are a great way to clog energy. It's like posting a stick in pure fluid water. It will collect moss to it over time. These rigid belief systems are like moss collectors in our energy field. If you want to know how a person becomes less fluid as an energy system, look at their beliefs.

The great thing about this understanding is that one can just free up their energy system by having an understanding of it as fluid energy. One limitation even open-minded people put on it is looking at it as two-dimensional. Those who use visualizations imagine energy coming into the top of the head and moving through the body. Even this is a limited belief system.

Energy is coming into us from all angles and all directions. It is more realistic to envision oneself as a car going through a car wash being permeated with water jets from all sides. Energy flows in from all directions and emanates out from us in all directions. We are more like a starburst in space than a stick figure moving through life like we are on a conveyor belt of time.

We are expansive, dynamic, multidimensional, expressive beings. The more we see ourselves this way, the more we can maintain a dynamic center that is not on any man made linear timeline. We are sovereign beings. As sovereign beings, we have no need to subjugate or diminish any other beings. This would cause them to be "clingy" to our energy field. No. We understand that to maintain a totally free orbit, we must allot this freedom to all others so they will not inadvertently impinge our freedom by bumping into our orbit. This is what aware souls do.

33 HOW TO BLESS SOMEONE

- Listen only to them when they speak without multitasking.

- Listen to them and really receive what they say instead of wandering in your head and thinking of what you are going to say next.

- Encourage them in what gets them excited without putting your perceived outcome on it.

- Accept a gift when they offer.

- Think kind things about them.

- See their potential.

- Envision them as beautiful and whole no matter what outer illusion depicts.

- Refuse to agree with them when they are self-deprecating.

- Look into their eyes when they speak.

- Pay attention to their tone and body language and hold them accountable for their truth.

- Refuse to compare them to anyone.

- Be excited for them.

- Be honest with them.

- Wish the best for them.

- Say only kind things about them.

- When someone else says anything derogatory about them, meet that person with dead silence.

- When you see something that they need or would enjoy, get it for them for no reason.

- See them manifesting the best possible version of themselves unequivocally.

- Abstain from weighing them down with your belief system.

- Allow them a bad mood without engaging it.

- Treat them as if they are an honored guest. They are. Imagine how lonely the world would be if we were here alone.

- Smile at them.

34 THE STILLNESS OF THE POND

There is no struggle. There is only us immersed in the serene setting of a beautiful moment. The belief that one can be anything BUT in the moment is what creates a rocking motion on the stillness of the pond. Flailing one's arms into the future using a rope of fear or trepidation or reaching to hook onto the past in the ways of regret is what creates the imbalances that one experiences.

If one would relax in the boat they are in, patiently tending the embers of the moment, they would realize that life is only the one moment. It is the one moment perpetually in play.

How do you know that you will survive?

You have thrived through eons of time.

How do you know you will be loved?

You, being an expression of life, are evidence enough.

How do you know you will be cared for?

Billions of particles of life move in complete synchronicity to carry nutrients to your brain, oxygen to your heart, and wellness to every corner of your beingness.

How do you know you matter?

Because you have the capability to uplift consciousness with the act of a simple smile.

One slight intention can shift the whole chemical makeup of another person simply by inducing them to smile.

Imagine what you are capable of doing when you realize your own worth and the power of the moment.

35 WAYS YOUR PET IS HEALING

When your pet steps all over you, they are actually stretching out connective tissue that is wrapped around your muscles and bones like cellophane. It can actually improve the mobility of your joints and muscles. It can even alleviate pain.

There are enzymes in your babies' saliva. When they lick your face, perhaps it can rejuvenate your skin.

When your cat purrs, it moves energy on a subtle level. Your cat's purr can help stagnant energy in your body move out. It is a form of jump starting issues in your body.

A person is supposed to have four hugs a day to stay healthy and balanced. Your pets are perpetual hugs. They provide all the physical contact we need.

Pets give us an incentive to get up out of bed and do what needs to be done. People can get in a funk. Your pet's needs will prevent you from staying in that funk. They need to be cared for. Our love for them, spills over into self-love.

Two energy systems share information. A stronger energy system can override the deficiencies of a weaker energy system. When you have young healthy pets, they can reprogram your body to youth and enthusiasm.

Pets are very compassionate beings. They absorb our pain as their own issues. People may never recognize how their pets have literally sacrificed their health and even their lives out of love for them.

Pets are a means of us giving ourselves love with one degree of separation. We will give and care for our pets in ways we refuse to give to ourselves. For many people who feel unworthy, this is an upgrade to teach them how to indirectly care for themselves.

Pets provide company. They prevent people from feeling isolated and alone. They show us compassion and offer a nonjudgmental environment, which is very healing.

Pets give us a sense of family. They add so much love and encouragement to our lives. Our pets think we are perfect. They allow us to be better than we believe we are. They are our children, best friends and even life partners. They fill in all the gaps when other humans fall short and fall through the cracks.

36 HOW TO RAISE YOUR FURRY FAMILY'S SELF-ESTEEM

- You don't own a pet; you are entrusted with someone's wellbeing.

- When interacting with your pet, realize that everything you imprint on them, whether kindness or indifference, will reflect in your pet's future incarnations.

- Talk to your pet. They get the gist of what you are saying.

- Don't tell their business to others; they appreciate a sense of privacy and may feel violated or embarrassed easily.

- Please stop telling their sad tale. They live in the moment. When you talk about their sad rescue, you force them to relive it. It is cruel.

- Please don't make fun of them or call them names. You are responsible for what they carry into their next incarnations. Are you going to send them along with scars or self-confidence?

- Please don't compare them to ones who have crossed. Each one is their own person. It is a lot of pressure to live in the shadow of someone else.

- When you adopt a new pet, please explain you are their forever home and mean it. Animals aren't disposable. The first question an animal asks when it has been sent from place to place is, " Can I stay?"

- If you contemplate re-homing a pet because of a behavioral issue, they will know that and it will acerbate the behavior. Most behavioral issues are on the part of the human for not understanding how to validate their pet.

- Pets look to their humans for subtle cues. They react when their people react. The calmer their people are, the calmer they tend to be. If your pet's behavior causes you to react, your pet will react to your reaction. That is how it goes.

- When walking a pet, realize that that time is THEIRS, not yours. They use that time to interact with others through sniffing. It is like you reading a magazine to relax. Please don't be selfish and pull them through the walk out of impatience. If you want a confident pet, allow them this time and get used to their pace. Don't pull them by the neck to your pace.

- Pets value their possessions. They give them a sense of security and self-identity. Please respect their items and don't pull them away from them like they don't care. They do.

- Your furry family enjoys a routine. It gives them a sense of security. They enjoy loving interaction. The more respectful of your pet you are, the more relaxed they will be.

- Don't allow children to use pets as a toy. If they pick up your pet when the pet is not engaged, show the child how that feels. When they are engaged in a project, pick THEM up and show them how irritating it is to be interrupted. Then gently explain that that is what they have been doing to kitty and that is why kitty runs away.

- Make yourself accessible to your pet at their level. If they are not allowed in your bed, get down on the floor with them once in awhile. That bonding time is so important. It helps them feel more like family and less disconnected.

- Dogs HATE to be separated from their pack. Realize that dogs don't know that they are safe when you put them in the back yard by themselves. They don't understand human boundaries. So they may feel exposed and vulnerable to the world. That is why they may be barking or anxious. They don't understand that they are safe when they are in a yard, even if it is fenced in. It can be really scary for them.

- Your relationship with your pet can be a reflection of your relationship with yourself. The better you treat your pet, the more you are reflecting self-love to yourself. In this way, loving your pet is very healing.

- Pets love and forgive. It is what they do. It is your job to allow them to love and not put them in a position to need to forgive.

37 HOW TO BE A GOOD LISTENER

- There is no multitasking when you listen to someone. Truly listening to someone entails catching energy that they are "throwing." To be distracted by other things is missing the "ball."

- Listen from the vantage point of the talker, as if these things could be happening to you. Otherwise, sheaths of opinions will block your ability to receive.

- When you talk to children, meet them at their level. If they have friends, treat them with respect too, even if they are stuffed or plastic.

- When someone is upset about something that seems silly, scan your own memory banks of a time you can remember feeling that way. This will help you to shut down in judgment.

- If you don't understand a point, don't nod and agree. This is disrespectful and dishonest. Simply interject that you are having trouble following the point they are making and ask for clarification.

- Don't indulge those who talk too much, complain too much or spew anger. Being a good listener is not a form of masochism.

- If you don't agree with someone, don't pretend to agree to be polite. This is actually rude because you are not honoring them enough to be honest. Just say, "I love you but I don't get that point." If it continues, then they don't respect you and you must honor yourself and shut down the interaction.

- If someone continuously drains you by wanting to use you to vent, talk about problems, complain, gossip or debate, then you are not listening to your own body that is telling you to remove yourself from this dynamic. If you do it because nobody else listens to them, you are being a martyr. The reason others are not listening to them is because it is not healthy for them. People literally make themselves sick by continually taking in low level vibrations this way.

- If you are forced into a situation where you have to be around a negative person, you can retrain them to be positive around you. When a person says negative things, ignore them and don't bite. Pretend you didn't even hear them. When they do get around to saying something positive, jump on it by engaging them. This is a means of rewarding them for positive behavior. This is how to retrain a human.

- Listen to your inner sensors like your "gut" or "heart" in regards to all matters. You will never lie to yourself, so never betray yourself by ignoring your truth. Listening to yourself is as important as listening to others.

- Always be truthful in a kind, pleasant way. Don't tolerate things just to avoid conflict or to prevent hurting someone's feelings. Your feelings matter too. You need to honor yourself as well as the other person. Truth resonates at a similar frequency as love so if you are just being polite and going through the motions, you are being less loving than if you are honest.

- People want to know how to communicate with animals. It is no different than communicating with people. When you put as much reverence into every interaction, every interaction will start to speak volumes. All of life will speak with you if your merely learn to listen in energy instead of in words.

- Our pets' problems may seem quaint but they are important issues to them. When your pet is hungry or wants a treat, it is no less important than when you are craving a snack. When they are sniffing out on their walk, realize that is their time to unwind and relieve stress. It is no different than you wanting to veg out in front of the TV. Realize what they are feeling before you just dismiss their issues.

- Listen to your inner promptings. They are truth trying to be heard. Never dismiss your dreams, passions, desires or hopes as a fancy. They are the precipice of a deep journey of awakening. Listening intently to the things that make you happy is dipping a toe into your omniscience.

- Encourage the impossible in others. Never be the dismal voice of reason. That voice has been used to squelch and diminish generation after generation. Be the one who people come to when they want to be encouraged or inspired. By doing this, you are someone's "break in the clouds."

- If you need wise council, sit under a tree. People don't understand the correlation between their own inspiration and what a tree is feeding them in assistance. The way to start making that connection is by spending time with a tree and seeing how your direction becomes more clear in doing so.

38 AN EXTENSION OF OUR OWN BEINGNESS

- Please stop telling yourself that you are bad in any derogatory way. Honor all aspects of yourself for their service to you. Please don't admonish them for doing their best.

- Fat cells are little soldiers protecting you from harm.

- The pain in your arm that is called carpal tunnel is your escape from doing time in a linear prison in a job you hate.

- Pain in your body is your way of opting out of a reality that is demanding and unkind.

- Being considered less beautiful was a choice you came in with so you could be considered at more than surface level. Perhaps you were sacrificed for your beauty and it is safer to have average appeal.

- Maybe being born with a disability was your way of learning lessons from a cruel world while opting out of the competition to be the best.

- Having medical issues is a great field study in compassion.

- Being born short is a literal means of changing your vantage point to gain awareness.

- Having one of your senses taken away is a means to awaken to your more empowering subtle senses.

- Losing someone is a means of realizing how to hold all your love dear within your realm.

- If we are born gay, perhaps we were dealt so much cruelty in being in a male or female body that the only way we can get our experiences with the opposite sex is within the safety of being the same sex.

- If we are transgender, perhaps we are the ones who have arrived at an awareness that does not have to compartmentalize our experiences to just identifying with one sex.

- Feeling the pain of others is an incredible gift of awareness of the reality of life.

- Being unappreciated by others is a way to glean self-love.

- Being hated within a family is a great way to meet your enemies up close and diffuse old grudges.

- Turning away from religion perhaps is a way to turn away from man-made law that has used God to manipulate the heart and will of the group consensus.

- Losing anything shifts one's vantage point from a complacency to being more present with life.

- Not attracting a mate, abundance, or certain experiences that we long for, may be something that we set up in a past life through the vows we have taken.

When we took vows in past lives, we took them forever and the effects of them may still be playing out.

- We are not being punished by our circumstances. We are being given incredible opportunities to thrive, awaken, gain flexibility and awareness to transcend. In transcendence, we realize that nothing was ever kept from us. That we were always able to benefit from it by seeing it in those around us. Everyone and everything that we witness is an extension of our own beingness. Realizing our relationship with them is a first step in our own empowerment.

39 DON'T WASTE ENERGY

Don't waste energy lamenting what you don't have. This is actually using your abilities to manifest and create lack. Take the passion out of it. Instead of dreaming of all the things you want, which creates a negative backwash, just visualize a lot of numbers in your bank account. It takes the negative charge of emotions out of your efforts and uses all the energy to manifest great numbers. If you can visualize having great things without going into the negative thoughts, then do that.

Allow your passion to lead you. Many of us will do for others what we don't feel worthy to do for ourselves. So use your intention to help others or the world to manifest abundance for yourself to use as a tool to help others.

Don't try to figure out the line to you and incredible wealth. That ability is above your pay scale. Just put your intention out into the Universe and allow the Universe to fill the request. Collect opportunities as you go without pinching the energy of them by prejudging. A penny on the ground is abundance. Accept it so that you can then practice accepting even more wealth.

Don't turn down payment. If someone wants to pay you, be ready to accept it. So many times, we will turn down payment in an act of generosity or unworthiness. What we are really stating is that we feel unworthy to be rich. We need to be generous to ourselves.

Expect payment for sharing your gifts. No one would expect a plumber to come to their house and fix their pipes because they have a natural talent as a plumber. They still deserve to be paid. This is true with your gifts, no matter how intangible they are. Others may not understand the ramifications of your assistance or how much work you put into what you do. You must be confident in what you do and the worth of what you share.

Skip the dance of feigning like you don't want to be paid when you actually do. If someone offers you money, it is a gift to honor you. Don't pretend that you don't want it. Accept the payment as appreciation and as a form of honoring yourself. You matter and your gifts are important.

Stop all derogatory remarks about rich people. If you are speaking about them in a negative way, it is a means of distancing yourself from them. If you don't like what rich people stand for, create incredible wealth for yourself and do incredible acts with the opportunity it affords.

Overshoot your goals. Instead of thinking millions, think billions.

Find a means to be around the frequency of abundance. Spend time in an affluent neighborhood in some way, work at a bank where you are handling money. Work at a high-end resort. Do whatever you can to be around the vibration of money.

Study the energy of money. Study rich people when you can. Do a field study on how they honor the things that they accrue with their wealth. Be around rich people as much as possible. Energy systems share energy. So be in the proximity of rich people so their energy system shares information with you through osmosis.

Stop being proud of being without. It is what many people have used to cope with not having. Some people demonize the rich and are pious about being poor. This mentality will keep you locked in the state that you are in. All judgment is diminishing, especially if it is pious in its righteousness.

Take care of the things that the Universe does bring to you. If you don't honor the things you have, how can you not be overwhelmed with having the responsibility of having a better quality of things? Keep everything that you have neat, tidy and well accounted for. That is a way of showing the Universe that you can be responsible to be the caretaker to more abundance and more things.

Being messy and throwing your things everywhere shows a total disregard for the abundance you already have. Nobody wants to give something to someone who is ungrateful. Throwing your things around is a way of showing ingratitude. Ingratitude closes your energy doorways. Being disrespectful of your possessions is a way of closing down your energy to having wealth and abundance.

Many people want abundance so they can hire others to help them, so be sure to honor all the people who do seemingly menial tasks and watch the care and reverence they put into it. As a wealthy person, you would be like an overseer to all these wonderful souls you would hire. Get an overview of all their reverence and respect for the details of their position so that you can adopt that reverence for the task of overseeing all those you will hire. It is no small matter.

Switch the messaging from being materialistic to one of honoring inanimate life. Rich people love things. Things are made of living atoms. Perhaps the way rich people honor things is a means to create abundance in itself. Perhaps what we have demonized as materialistic is a way of leading us all away from wealth. Perhaps the whole key to having wealth is to honor things as those who are non-materialistic honor Nature. Perhaps it is those of us who brag about being non-materialistic who are the ones that have missed the mark. Perhaps we are the ones who are bigoted against non-animate life. Adopt a stance of loving life in all forms and seeing inanimate life as an extension of Nature. All the materials to make everything came from Nature anyway. Perhaps this one thing is the key to attracting more abundance into all lives.

40 STOP THE MADNESS

The reason for disease that trumps all others is treating the body like an inanimate object with no feelings. This is wrong and barbaric. Every component of our body has consciousness. This means that it cares about surviving.

- It feels rejection,
- it gets overwhelmed,
- it cries in pain,
- it wants to be validated,
- it wants to be loved,
- it wants to do a good job,
- and it wants to be appreciated.
- It also wants its love felt and its contribution acknowledged.

The body parts have similar reactions to being ignored and invalidated that you do.

- It shuts down,
- acts out,
- screams out,
- feigns sickness,

- gives up,
- hides,
- mopes,
- sabotages the ingrate,
- sabotages others,
- holds resentment,
- builds up anger,
- drags along for attention,
- sabotages others,
- tries harder,
- exhausts itself.

So when body parts are being invalidated by us and suffering, instead of pouring love, kindness and compassion into them, we...

- Complain about them,
- cut them out,
- poison them,
- eradicate them with radiation,
- mutilate them,
- blame them for the whole system being out of whack,

- talk about how they aren't functioning,
- continue to demoralize them and
- curse them for our misgivings.

I have such compassion for a body. Self-worth is a tough one, but the way a group of cells holds together with all the ingratitude and ignorant practices that are thrown at it is amazing. Every body is an unsung hero in my books. When someone is complaining about something their body has failed at, I talk silently with their body and give them compassion for what they have to endure at the hands of ignorance.

Body parts are living, breathing, contributing organisms just like all aspects of nature are functioning individuals working in agreement with the ecosystem that each is a part of. For optimal health, everyone should start thinking of their body as a community of souls working for a common goal instead of thinking of it as one overlord being served by the minions. In doing so, you give so much of yourself voice and reason. This creates fluidity in the functioning of your body systems rather than stagnant pools of energy that cause dissension or disease in the whole.

41 IMPORTANT FACTS ABOUT TREES

Trees communicate through their rooting system. It is similar to how we communicate through social media. We needed the understanding of how computers interact to understand how trees communicate. Until social media, there was no tangible reference point available.

Trees not only exchange carbon dioxide for pure air, they also exchange stagnant, negative thoughts for clarity and inspiration. Trees prevent people from being unbalanced because they take in all the stagnant energy (like they would fertilizer), that holds people in negative thought and emotional patterns. They give them clarity of purpose and reason in exchange.

Trees love their children. They look after their children from their vantage point. If you care for a tree's sapling, they will be contented and appreciative as if they are feeling it as well.

Trees don't really die. They just go deep into the ground and come up again as a sapling.

The rings on a tree depict all the stagnant energy they have taken in from the environment and the people around them.

Trees induce sanity, calm and reason into people. The areas in the world that have fewer trees are the ones that depict more of a violent temperament.

Trees are not motionless. They undulate. Thinking they are motionless is a trick of the mind that has been instilled generation upon generation of human conditioning. If you sit and stare at a tree for a long time, you will see how they really move. It can be alarming, if not intimidating, at first. In a past era, there was a genocide of all those who could interact with trees. This was done to instill the Christian god. It left the psyche of those who loved trees paralyzed in a fear of interacting with them. That is what is being addressed now by reminding everyone of how special trees are.

When no one communicates with a tree, the tree "checks out" and spends most of its attention pulled away from the surface. They interact among themselves like humans spending all their time on social media. That is partly why they seem so lifeless to us. But if you engage a tree, they are happy to come to the surface and interact with you.

Trees are responsible for most of the inspiration that humans receive. Many of the heartfelt songs and poetry that people have written have actually been downloaded into them by the trees.

The ability to communicate with trees is an aspect of female or yin energy. In ancient civilizations, it was normal to interact with trees and to seek their council. A big part of the desecration of Goddess energy has been to demonize those who communicate with trees. It past eras, there was a genocide committed on those who were able to interact with trees. There is a memory of this today in the way society demonizes tree huggers. The more you honor and respect trees openly, the quicker the planet will be healed.

Respecting and honoring trees is a direct gauge as to how humanity is auto correcting itself after male energy has systematically tried to annihilate female empowerment. But what people are starting to understand is that it is not men against women. Each human is compiled of both male and female energy. So to honor and respect trees creates a balance and an upgrade within our own energy system.

Trees are not fearful of storms. They don't fear dying like humans do. When there is a storm brewing, there is an electricity and excitement in the air. That electric feeling is the trees' excitement about the rainfall. It is their "Celebratory Feast." Notice that electricity happens after a dry spell. When it is a huge storm brewing, the trees are very excited.

When there is a forest fire, the animals seem to know miles away to get out of the way of danger because the trees warn them.

Forest Fires are a tree's way of burning off the negativity in the world. There is a lot of negativity being burned off right now. It is part of the way they have been providing balance to the world. If you don't want wild fires, teach people to stop hating.

Trees are spirit guides. They really do look out for people. In lanes of highway that overlook a road, the trees are familiar with the people who drive to work and drive home at night. They find it fascinating that humans drive home so heavy after a day at work. The trees absorb that negativity for them as they drive by. That is why driving down a tree-lined road is so enjoyable.

Trees consider themselves part of the family. That cozy, nurturing feeling that you have in your home is a tree looking out for you and exuding comfort.

If you want an edge in life or need to feel more security, ask the trees to help you. If you are looking to buy a home in a competitive market or an impossible situation, ask the trees in the new property to help you. They can open and block energetic passageways more than is realized.

Trees think humans are amusing; they cut down a grove of them and then replant a row of trees after they have just cut a bunch of them down. Trees think humans are ridiculous in how they need to control nature in this way.

Trees don't understand boundaries like property lines. They don't realize that they are considered to be owned by the person in the nearest house. They love and nurture all the humans around, not just the ones who believe they own them.

Trees love to share their gifts. When you eat fruit right off a tree, the tree can then experience consciousness through your eyes. It is a form of them understanding humans better. This bond between humans and trees has been desecrated by the way that trees are treated like slaves in an orchard rather than receiving gratitude for what they provide. Trees in an industrial orchard find it more difficult to pour their love into their fruit because of the way they receive no appreciation for what they give. This love that is not present is a form of enzyme to the body of humans. That is why some fruits and vegetables cause heartburn. They were grown and harvested with a lack of gratitude.

Trees enjoy when a branch of theirs is invited into a home as decoration when it has dropped off accidently. They then get to see what it is like in the home and they send that information back to the main tree. This is how trees learn from interacting with us.

Trees are devastated when they are cut down by the whims of ignorant humans who plop them in their homes and celebrate as the life force drains out of them. Such ignorance saddens them.

Trees are excited that I share this information. They are excited about being able to inspire and interact with humans again. As more people interact with trees, a renaissance will ensue. This creative energy that is returning to the planet will dry up a lot of the hate, greed and power mongering that is prevalent, presently. If you want to change the world, connect with your local trees and reignite the wisdom of the trees back into the planet.

42 WAYS TO SHUT DOWN YOUR ENERGY FIELD

- Defer to someone else that you don't agree with.
- Allow yourself around people who don't honor you.
- Do what you are told.
- Agree with the outer state of affairs.
- Lament about the past.
- Have disapproval for yourself.
- Be overcritical.
- Be afraid.
- Accept the things that don't seem right in the world.
- Feel helpless.
- Play the victim.
- Lie.
- Say you will do something and then not follow through. At first, this will dilute your energy, but then it will have to shut it down.
- Watch negative entertainment.
- Be around angry people.

- Obsess over finding a partner.

- Ignore your own instincts.

- Remove yourself from Nature.

- Have unkind intentions towards anyone.

- Harbor resentment or jealousy.

- Overdo anything.

- Engage in recreational substances habitually. At first, they will seem to open your energy and this will be the draw, but you can't maintain this synthetically and will be forced to shut down. This can feel like being slammed against a wall.

- Take everything too personally.

- Fixate on what others are doing.

- Obsess over current affairs.

- Retire the things that bring you pleasure like hobbies and natural abilities.

- Buy into outmoded belief systems, such as aging is inevitable.

- Expect that negative things are inevitably looming towards you, like disease.

- Try too hard.

- Think too much.

- Get caught up in drama.

- Programming unworthiness and the false concept of humility.

- Compete to feel worthy.

- Staying immersed in the linear world. This causes you to be trapped in a linear belief system that encompasses all of the above.

43 WHAT IS CAUSING YOUR MOOD?

Every negative thought, fear, twinge of anger or belief that comes to you is an opportunity to challenge it and move on or recoil into a lesser state of freedom. As something comes into your psyche, challenge where it came from. Ask yourself what transaction created or uncovered this?

Was it the chemicals in your food or even the consciousness of the components that sacrificed themselves for this meal?

Was it the indifference of the workers who cooked the meal, packaged the ingredients, or delivered it to your table?

Was it an exchange that happened with a friend?

Is someone that you care about going through something and you opened a window to their pain through sympathy or sadness?

Is it someone using you to strengthen their case in a discussion?

Did watching something on TV manipulate your emotions for entertainment or trigger a past life?

Is some group using you as a pawn to pass an agenda or strengthen their position in the world?

Are your emotions being manipulated for the gain of some political party?

Is someone profiting off of your devoted stance?

Is your faith, loyalty, devotion or integrity being challenged to draw you closer into a group consensus?

Are fears being triggered to keep you loyal to a group and triggering the primal urge to belong?

Are you going deeper into your own realms of self-awareness and naturally releasing all that is not truly you?

Are you realizing who you are beyond all the confines of articulation?

You are an individual atom of love in the heart of God. Nothing anyone can say or do can remove you from your true essence. Everything that challenges you is meant to strengthen your awareness of yourself as a continually awakening, loving being.

Here is your proof: Even when everything around you seems hopeless and gloomy, you never lose your ability to know yourself as loving and kind at the core, right? That is because you are love at the core. All else is the illusion that outer conditions have tried to put on you. You are only loving if...You can only be special if...You only matter if.... NO! Those are all lies!

This is the time to reject the lies and accept the beauty and wonder of who you are: Love and loved beyond all outer feelings, beliefs and circumstances. This is the time to accept your rightful place in the heart of love and demonstrate love as your mainstay. By doing so, you defy all that has tried to define or diminish you. You prevail as pure love.

44 WAYS WE CURSE OTHERS

A curse is merely circumventing someone's direction with your own intention. It is not necessarily an ominous thing. Many curses are done by our loved ones too. Here are ways we curse others:

- Deem them sad. Sad is a form of energetic quicksand. When you say someone is sad, it is difficult to get out of.

- Diminish their dreams.

- Say things like: "You will never find anyone who will love you like I do," "You will never amount to much if you don't...," or "You will starve as a musician."

- Compare them to someone you resent as in, "You look just like your father (your ex)."

- When they are telling you about something important to them, you interject a story about yourself.

- You compare their accomplishments with your own or someone you know.

- You compare them to anyone.

- You secretly judge them.

- You put expectations on them.

- You secretly believe they are not capable.

- You gossip about them.

- You talk about them when they are not around.

- You baby them when they are not living up to their potential.

- When they share something that is important to them, you put an opinion on it.

- When they share their truth, you argue a point with them.

- You ignore them.

- You inadvertently don't hear what they are saying.

- You secretly have an opinion of them.

- You rank them in importance to you.

45 HOW TO SAY F#@K YOU TO SOMEONE

- Be late.

- Ignore them.

- Pretend to be listening when you are "multitasking."

- Compare them to someone else.

- When they are sharing, turn the conversation to be about you.

- Make them feel like you are doing them a favor by fitting them in to your schedule.

- When they share something, quote someone else as an expert.

- Dump your issues on them.

- Expect them to do something for you without an equal energy exchange in return.

- Forget to say thank you.

- Rank them in order of their importance to you behind family and BEST friend.

- Allow others to talk about them to you.

- Act like you are doing them a favor by spending time with them.

- Share their concerns with others.

- Have expectations of them.

- Talk about them behind their back.

- Think or say anything derogatory about whatever or whomever they hold dear.

- Feel they are replaceable.

- Hold an upper hand in the relationship.

- Be polite instead of telling them the truth.

How to Show Reverence to All Life Through Your Interactions with Others:

- Be present when you say you show up.

- Listen intently when they speak and not think of other things in your head. That is not even being with them.

- Allow the moment to be about them. Let them shine to their greatest heights without putting the glass ceiling of someone else on them.

- Allow the whole conversation to be about them. Learn to get joy in helping them shine.

- Consider it an honor to be with them. It is. It is such a miracle to be with others. Realize how lonely it would be to be on the planet alone.

- Treat them like an original that no one has figured out yet. Allow all their experiences to be unique. They are to them.

- Learn to process your issues in a way that is not spewing energy onto them. If it comes out once in a while, consider it a great gift that they took this from you, but don't make it a habit.

- Appreciate every nuance of the relationship, even the parts that bring your issues to the surface. They are doing you a favor by not allowing them to stay buried.

- Be grateful that there are others to engage with, who see your splendor in some way, and return the favor by seeing theirs.

- Look beyond the physical, emotional and mental limitations of your friends to see them as those bright shining starbursts they are within. This will help them bring those qualities out.

- Hold every interaction as if it is a sacred union with the Universe. Because it is.

- Revel in the dance you are allowed to partake of with all life. If someone steps on your toes, realize they are merely learning the steps of the intimate dance with life.

- Know that everyone who comes into your realms was sent there with a divine purpose. Honor that purpose even if they are not able to.

- See everyone as an equal to your highest self. That is the true definition of humility.

- Speak only truth to others because truth and love resonate at similar frequencies. If you are afraid to do that, then you are lacking love because fear is the opposite of love.

- Honor every atom of life in its quest to perfection, knowing that perfection is not a sterile state but a random, seemingly chaotic weave of action and bliss woven into the cloth of humanity.

- Allow others' differences to unabashedly bump against you and shake off some of the rust within your own depth.

- Revel at the inconveniences, awkwardness and random experiences that others bring to you. This is all while refusing to be pulled out of your center with any dysfunction. How else will you strengthen the timber of your own orbit?

- Be able to pour genuine praise and recognition out as easily as you used to share blame.

- Be bold and gregarious in defending your own unique flair, and by doing so, invite others to embrace their own.

- Be still in your judgment, gracious in your praise, and awakened in your interactions with all life.

- Transport your awareness into whomever you are interacting with and switch your vantage point from you to them. In that exercise, you can develop true empathy and you will be mastering the art of listening.

- If anyone says anything unkind to you, watch the reaction in your energy field. Your energy will want to shut down and shoot energy back as an insult or respite. Master the art of being non-reactive. Allow the sting of their assault to pass through you and maybe strip off a layer that is no longer useful. That is all it is when someone hurts you; their comment is ripping off a layer of the ego. Allow it to go! Rejoice at the freedom.

- Choose who, what, when, why and how you engage others. Otherwise, you are punishing them for a past transgression when you were held captive. This is what passive-aggressive is.

- Love, sing, rejoice passionately whether you are alone or among others. Allow everyone to see your genuine self as encouragement for them to show you theirs.

- See beyond all differences to the similarities. All beings are energy and have a heart. Even single cells have consciousness. Love each atom of life by pouring kindness and gratitude into every mitochondria of every single cell. That way you can leave judgment out of it. Who can't love one cell? Then love one cell a billion trillion times.

46 WORDS AND PHRASES THAT SHOULD BE RETIRED

Saying something is *sad*. It is a form of cursing a situation and putting yourself at a higher moral ground.

Stepchild.

Half brother or sister.

Rescue pet. No animal wants to be referred to as the perpetual victim. It keeps them in that state of disadvantage.

"*My + anything negative.*" The word, "my" glues the situation to you instead of allowing it to pass through and release. Some pain is leaving, not coming in. When you say "my," it stays.

"Father" in referring to God. It is a direct reflection of how women are treated unequally in the world. Of course, if God is a man, woman would be less important. Good thing That was just a depiction of Source during the dark ages. If man can upgrade his technology every few months, why can't he upgrade his concept of God?

Pet names like "honey," or "sweetie." These are meant to give you leverage over someone. That is why waitresses say them, perhaps, so they don't have to feel like servants while taking care of your needs in a restaurant. The pet names leverage the dynamics.

Left or right as far as describing Americans. It is insulting to be pigeonholed and fought over like we are ignorant pawns. When we fall into those labels for politicians' convenience, we are giving up our rights to be seen as individuals.

Labels of any kind. Labels are for those who don't perceive in energy. It is a quick reference point to identify something or someone that you don't really see, but can feel around for in the dark and then move on. Labels make it too easy to discount others. People deserve to be seen.

"Sorry" in every day vernacular. People who say they are sorry habitually are reliving something in their past that they feel guilty for. They are usually insecure, or feel unworthy in some way and are apologizing for existing. Saying sorry a lot wilts the spirit.

When something good happens, saying that it is unbelievable. This is a way to cap other good things from getting through and reassuring yourself that this awesome event is a one time deal and not a usual occurrence.

Blanket statements, like "people are all selfish," or "the world is a mess." This is actually a way of cursing all people and the world. Whenever we make a blanket statement, we are putting a glass ceiling on the subject of that statement.

Overgeneralizations. These are definite glass ceilings on the subject as well. Conformity depends on enough people agreeing with these generalizations to keep everyone energetically locked in them. That is why labels are so important to power mongers. They are the ones that use them most. Notice people who want control in government make the overgeneralization of saying, "the American people" when they answer. This is a calculated form of minimizing them. Everyone should be angry when they hear this statement and say to themselves, "you do not speak for me!"

Agreeing with anything you don't really agree with. This is a way of betraying your energy. It is a way of giving to a cause that you don't agree with. Why would you do that? Bigotry and most prejudices are perpetrated this way.

Negative statements. They create negative outcomes.

Derogatory self-talk. This merely is an attack from within and it is painful for people who love you to watch.

Expressing of defeating attitudes. The fifth dimension is fueled by love and kindness. The more positivity we see, the more evidence in a shift in consciousness everyone will experience.

Insults. They are residual energy of a negative world. It is a subtle attempt for negative energies to goad us back into a negative world. We are too good for that.

Anger is a pent up energy that needs to be released. Energy is neutral when it flows naturally, but when it is pent up, it has to be released, like steam on a boiling kettle. When people are moving, creating, thinking, imagining, and caring about others, the energy is flowing nicely. Resentment is merely backed up energy. Figure out how to release it. Sometimes speaking truth or doing a kindness gets the energy flowing again.

Demonizing names for wonderful things like tree hugger, bleeding heart, cat lady. There are positive attributes of these things and implying they are imbalanced is preventing kindness from being accepted or expected in the world. Kind people need to be protected. Kindness is an upgrade.

47 HOW TO REMOVE YOURSELF FROM LINEAR LIMITATIONS

Life is like a netting of illusion. Thinking about the past or worrying about the future pulls the drawstring of the netting around you more. It is an energetic way of ensuring yourself you will never lose the security of your netting.

Immersing yourself in the moment is a way of loosening the drawstring on the netting and allowing a big enough opening to remove yourself. If you practice this enough, it allows the netting to fall away.

This is what meditation was supposed to achieve for people. But many people merely use the practice as a means of tolerating the netting. The fabric of the netting is made up of the same mind energy that is used in meditation. It is difficult to differentiate the resolve from the thing that contains us.

There are many ways to remove yourself from linear existence and expound yourself into an exponential reality.

Do things you love. Anything that gets you lost in the moment is actually pulling you out of time and space. Love itself melts away the netting and allows all things to be possible. We have been led to deduce love as a corny concept because of its concentrated power to free us as individuals and all of humanity as well. Each individual has the capability of changing the world with their love if only they have the capacity and capability to do so. A great technique is to consciously practice loving all the people, species and atoms in the world. It is easier to do if you imagine the world as smaller as a means to wrap your head and heart around it.

Visualizations and using the imagination are dynamic means of stepping out of the netting. If done consistently, one can be the commander of the netting instead of trapped in it. This is what creative geniuses do. The possibilities are available to all.

Don't nail down your life in time. Every time you make an appointment, you are nailing yourself into time and space. It is necessary to make some appointments to function in this linear world, but the more you can leave your calendar open, the more free you will be.

Don't fill your intentions with empty promises. If you say you are going to do something, ensure that you do it. When you don't, you split your energy in two paths: the you that walks around, and the intention you set out. The more you send out false intentions, the more you dilute your effectiveness in life. You will end up showing up merely as a projection screen image in life and not really being immersed in it. Your energy will literally have no integrity. Integrity is having your intentions and you always on the same page. It is a dynamic, effective person who does this.

Stop talking and thinking about the past. Stop talking and worrying about the future. Thoughts are like little barbs that hook us into the netting of illusion. They are what tangle us up, instead of allowing us freedom in our own beingness. Feelings clip us in as well. The more you can catch yourself being in the past or future, the more you can bring yourself into the present. The present is the portal to expound.

Question everything you have been told to believe. Most of our conditioning has been to keep us immersed in a linear form of slavery. Pay attention to how much you have been conditioned to move along in life like it is a conveyor belt: birth to death, nine to five, season to season. When you follow the mandates of conditioning, you are on autopilot and not free to expound. This is why creative types seem so non-committal. They are.

Stop thinking of life and death with such division. Heaven is not a place. It is a state of consciousness. It is a vibration that overlays this one, yet at a more subtle frequency. When someone dies, they merely drop the coarse vibration of this world and then exist at the finer frequency. They are still themselves as much as ever and are so much closer than we fathom. They are right outside that netting of illusion of a linear reality. This netting is what prevents us from connecting with them.

Be grateful. Gratitude is a physiological process of opening your chakras to receive more energy. They open like an aperture of a camera. It isn't emotions that open them. It is the greater flux of energy that gives us the warm feeling when grateful. It is a physiological process. We use emotions as a shortcut to do this. But if someone has a hard time mocking up gratitude, perhaps they will have better luck merely setting the intentions to consciously open up the chakras. This will bypass the need to be emoting gratitude.

Talk less. Talking is filled with all these barbs that keep us immersed in the netting. I personally exist without the netting on as much as possible. When I listen to others, it is a means of being wrapped in the netting. When you talk about problems, you are giving the coordinates of them in time and space and sending others to that misery. It is pretty low on the survival scale to do this. It is how we have been trained to keep each other trapped.

Even light workers are limited by linear existence. When you visualize energy coming in the top of your head and out your feet, this is a linear understanding of energy. Energy is pouring into you on all sides and at all angles at all times. You are not a solid body but an emanating starburst of energy. The more you see yourself sending out and receiving love and beautiful intentions in every direction, the more you will grasp a higher concept of yourself.

Every time you label yourself, you are nailing yourself in time and space. At one time, we all perceived in energy. It is a more subtle but more accurate awareness. Not perceiving in energy is a form of being blind. Labels are a way for those who are blind to feel around in the dark for what they are looking for. That is why, the more unaware someone is, the more there is a need for labels. The unaware depend on labels to find their way around. Labels are also a way that groups keep us in the sheep mentality. They use labels to keep us blind and therefore, easier to control. When a group is hell bent on using a label, realize that they are really hell bent on control.

When you breathe, you are not merely inhaling and exhaling. You are communing with all of life. You are sending out from your energy field atoms of life imprinted with your unique vantage point. You are sharing all that you are with the Universe. In return, you accept in all the information it has to give you, which is imprinted in the atoms of air you take in. In this exchange, we are exchanging the information and vantage point of all beings. There is much wisdom in our breath. We would benefit from being consciously aware of that as a means of better digesting the information we receive. It is little different from conscious eating.

48 IF YOU THINK LIFE IS THROWING EVERYTHING IT CAN AT YOU...

IT IS!!! You are exactly right. It is. But it is temporary. It is pushing all humanity through the process of enlightenment. It is all okay. You are fine. You are breathing. You are loving and you are aware. The fact that you are being assaulted PROVES your value. You can get through this.

If you practice being grateful under any condition, you are strengthening your energy systems to work against their primal instinct to close. THAT IS ALL THAT MASTERSHIP IS. That is it. Regret and worry close the chakras and dry up the connection to Light and Love. If you can stay centered and keep the chakras open amongst the barrage and onslaught, you are golden. Literally! I promise.

It is that simple. To say it is difficult is to give into the bullshit. We can do this! We can bring Joy, Love, Abundance, Freedom. Health and Wholeness back to the land. We are all beacons, and when more are all lit up, we will allow all of humanity to ignite.

49 RESPECTING INANIMATE LIFE: THE SECRET TO HAVING

All of life is made up of living atoms, even the inanimate objects that we are surrounded by every day. If they are made up of living atoms, they have consciousness. They are alive. When a group of atoms collects together in the form of an item, they form a group consciousness. This group consciousness can be considered their soul.

I have been researching inanimate life to bring understanding to the world as to why we are not in greater accord living here. Because I am receptive to understanding, inanimate life has been speaking to me, in a sense, to give me greater understanding. This greater understanding can be added to the group consciousness of humanity and can bring greater awareness to all individuals.

That is what happens when anyone makes a discovery that uplifts humanity. It is similar to running the four-minute mile. Once it was impossible, but now it is very doable. This is how we expand the consciousness of man. This would be happening more currently, but billionaires have been buying up innovations that would take away their competition in industries like coal. They have been dumbing down humanity for their own gain.

I was watching the news about the aftermath of hurricane Irma. I kept seeing newscasters make off-handed comments on things that had been strewn about. There was a broken washing machine or a refrigerator. They had been tossed and battered by the storm. But to me, they were dead bodies. They had been killed by the storm as readily as people were. I don't expect people to develop the sensitivities I have overnight. But from my vantage point of respecting all life, the loss of their life was something to have reverence for as well.

There is so much information here to awaken the consciousness of man. I understand the ridicule it could induce. I don't care. People who don't value life in all forms are missing an aspect of self-love and the possibility to expand their awareness so much more.

I have been contemplating on inanimate life and it has been giving me insights. I was making my bed today and the blankets just seemed to fall into place themselves. They had. The blankets seem to be telling me that the more respect that is given to inanimate life, the more it cooperates with humans. People who kick the car and abuse their things are working against themselves. My bedding felt very respected today and helped me lay it on the bed nicely.

I know my house has a consciousness. That feeling of being glad to be home is mutual. I feel my house greeting me when I get home. It loves that I know it as a living being and I never say anything demeaning about it. Someone once insulted my house saying it should be torn down and rebuilt. I chided that person for their insensitivity. I would never talk about anyone that way.

When my car died, it was very sad to have it be taken to the scrap yard. I did not want its soul to be left there feeling unloved and abandoned. So I did a little ceremony before the tow truck driver came. I transferred the soul of my car into the house temporarily. When a friend found me another used car to drive, I infused the soul of the old car into it as well. It was astounding to see that even though it was another make and model, it looked exactly like the last one. After I transferred the soul of my last car into the new car, it suddenly felt comfortable to me. After that, there was no unfamiliar feeling about the car.

Another piece of insight I received from inanimate wisdom was about rich people. Is being rich really about money, or is something greater happening? I saw on Oprah once how rich people take good care of their things. They love things. Maybe rich people have so many nice things because they love and respect things. We have demonized them for being materialistic. But we have also demonized those who love trees and those who advocate for peace.

So maybe we should revisit the possibility that being materialistic is a form of respecting all life. Maybe those who have less have lost their ability to respect the items around them and infuse their feelings of lack into them. Maybe in that way, items sort of choose to be with a human who respects them. Perhaps the way to gain more abundance is to show a deep gratitude and respect for inanimate life. Maybe that is the key to attracting more things into our world.

50 THINGS TO KNOW WHEN A LOVED ONE IS READY TO CROSS OVER

Getting ready to cross is a very personal time. Talking about someone's health issue, bodily functions or story is a desecration to their person. People do this at first to convey information, but then to get attention from it, and then out of a repetitive habit. It really is nobody's business. People want to know details but almost all of wanting to know is lascivious in some way. It is a very private time.

Some people resent those who are quiet during this time. That is their coping mechanism. They may have a better understanding of the process than one who is trying to keep busy all the time. If someone is quiet, please respect that. It is their sacred prerogative.

Talking about the person crossing in the third person is an overt violation of their personhood. Many people take great pride in doing this. It is like they are proud of having a role of domination over this dynamic person who was once larger than life. Talking to the doctors or others in front of them about them is passive aggressive. It is like saying, "I am important now and you are not anymore." At the least it is disrespectful.

Talking about the person as if they are well and not experiencing something profound is a form of denial. It is a coping mechanism for those not emotionally ready to accept a shift in their world of losing this presence. It is invalidating though to the person who is fighting for their life. Please don't tell them, "they are just fine and going to beat this," when it is common knowledge that they aren't. This is isolating for the individual preparing to cross who wants to just feel close to their loved ones at that time.

No need to fill up space with mindless chatter. Some patients may want to hear about mundane things but others may want to enjoy the silence. Silence is not a bad thing. When someone is working on crossing over, silence is very pleasant and it helps them tune into the vibration that they are acclimating to.

All the drama is self-indulgent. Removing ourselves from the physical body is a very natural process. We have done it infinite times. Be grateful for the transition time of illness that allows your loved one to do this on their terms with the ability to say goodbye. Crossing over is a simple matter of slipping out of the physical body and adjusting to the new vibration of the astral plane. We are evolved enough to tune into this vibration as a species but control factions have prevented it. Those who use their imagination and are creative may more easily tune into the vibration of the astral plane. Those who are rigid and conforming may have a harder time with someone crossing.

The process of crossing over is really simple and pleasant. It is more traumatic to be born than it is to leave the physical realm.

Death is a naïve notion inflicted on man to control his behavior in society. It works. There is a direct correlation between a group's belief-system and to how adamantly they are in controlling others. We do not die. We attain our awareness and keep accruing the ability for love and compassion lifetime after lifetime. All of life is an exercise in stretching our capacity to love.

Using a person's illness to get attention is very low on the survival scale. People who do this stand out as having little understanding or compassion for the one who is actually going through the process of crossing over. Talking about someone who is ill just to indulge yourself is a violation of spiritual law and desecrates the person you talk about.

When it is someone's time to cross and they have accepted it, the best thing you can do is show your gratitude for knowing them and give them permission to cross. Many times the people in the physical are holding the one who is ready to cross back from their journey. It is very difficult for the one crossing when people do this. We do this to our pets too. It is self-indulgent to pray for them to stay or have prayer circles to get them well after the point they are gearing to cross. This is such a personal thing and the person may not have the strength to say it out loud because they don't want to upset their loved ones. But it is self-indulgent to keep them here. It is a violation of their sacred essence. It is also a huge violation to start a prayer circle for them. Many people who do this are merely gleaning attention from their spiritual group for themselves.

Don't put your concepts of the process of crossing onto the individual. Imagery and belief systems are very personal and can be limiting to a person who has different reference points. You may think it is the most beautiful imagery to say that "God will meet you at the door." But they may have different imagery and think of God as vengeful. It may conjure up imageries of past life crossings of the angel of death looming nearby. It may induce fear in them that is counter-productive. Allow people to have their experience in crossing and don't put the limitations of your belief system on them unless they ask.

Crossing over is very natural. The person stays in tune with the body for about three days and there can be a great connection made with them at this time. Being fixated in despair can block this subtle communication which is frustrating to the one who has crossed because they are eager for you to know how great they are doing and to reassure you that everything is fine.

When you go to sleep, you are able to slip out of the physical body and visit your loved one in their new life that can, many times, look similar to their life on earth. There will, though, be much more freedom. You have a great time visiting with them and when you wake up, because of your limiting belief systems, don't remember that you have just had a great time with your loved one. They get exasperated in seeing you sad when you wake up. Sometimes you have a good laugh with them about how silly the beliefs are here on earth. But then you wake up and forget.

The person who has crossed is able to manipulate electricity or induce a song to play to mean something to you. They want you to know they are fine. They still are working to comfort you. There will be a sign from nature, the wind, or one of their familiar phrases said out of the mouth of a stranger. But this takes effort for them. It would be so much easier for our loved ones who have crossed if an initial understanding of the process was in place. It would make it easier for them to connect and offer comfort if death wasn't immersed in so much mystery.

Talking about what led to your loved one's death, locks them into the traumatic experience. It pulls on them from the other side and distracts them from their joy in the moment. This is true with our pets as well. That is why Native Americans never talk about those who have crossed over. They know it is an insult to them. They understand that our loved ones come back to us in the bodies of our babies. That is why they respect their children so much. They knew and recognized them as their forefathers.

Your loved ones will also come back to the family if there are strong bonds to do that. You can look for them in the eyes of your children, nieces and nephews and even grandchildren.

When someone has taken their own life, they immediately realize that they have made a mistake. They are taken through a process of understanding that is horrific compared to what they were trying to escape on earth. Immediately, they will pull on friends and family members that they left behind. That is why there is such a balm of despair over the home of someone who has committed suicide. They are trying to relieve their anguish by inflicting it on those who love them.

Many times they will compel others to take their life to keep them company. If someone takes their own life, you have to cut off all connection and sympathy to them. It is self-survival. You can't help them. It is tough love and they need to take their "medicine." Having sympathy or guilt for them can be used to psychically manipulate you and can destroy the happiness of whole families. It is best to focus your attention on the ones who are here with you in that case. It really is self-survival because hardly anyone is equipped to deal with such an energy as one who has ended their own physical life.

When you cross over, you don't magically attain super powers and transform into a cosmic angel. You can give little insights to someone who loves you, but you do not become omniscient merely by crossing over. It is a lateral move. One woman thought her drug dealing brother who committed suicide was now her guardian angel. He merely used her to satiate his cravings for drugs, alcohol and cigarettes. She though it was funny she took up smoking after he died. Once she understood why, she could wean herself off of them.

Your pets love you but are so "in the moment." When they go outside, and you get very upset, it induces the belief in them that they have crossed over and are in another life. They may leave you behind when that happens. It is important that you depict calm and loving thoughts to your pets, especially when they are lost or going through a procedure. When it is time for them to cross, the most loving thing you can do is stay in a loving state with them and not talk about or relive their trauma. This can be a form of hell for them because every time you talk about them getting hit by the car, they are forced to relive it. By keeping your thoughts pleasant and loving, you are demonstrating the greatest love possible. Drama and sadness do not register well on our pets. It doesn't actually register well on people either.

51 HOW ADOPTING REINCARNATION UNIVERSALLY WILL SAVE THE WORLD

People will realize they could come back in any situation. This will cause them to want to improve the quality of life for all to hedge and increase their odds of having a favorable future incarnation

The earth, water and land will be cared for better because people will realize that they want to preserve the quality of life for their future incarnations.

People will not be able to use birth control rights to try to enslave women. They will realize that there is no such thing as murder to the unborn. They simple incarnate in another vessel.

People will adopt accountability in dealing with others. They will realize that no amount of lies or throwing money and power at a situation will save them from the consequences they create for themselves.

People will be kinder to others. They will be able to tap into their experiences in past lives when they learned compassion, instead of feeling and acting beyond reproach as an island to themselves.

Children will be treated with much respect and reverence as people realize, like the Native Americans do, that our children are our forefathers coming back to be with us.

There will not be such drama around the concept of death. People will not feel cut off from their loved ones who have moved on. They will realize that those they love will return to them soon enough.

Life will be more fluid because people will not feel so contained in their human vessel. They will realize that it is only the big toe of their consciousness. So they will be more curious to explore their total self.

Written mandates will not be so written in stone as people realize their fluidity and flexibility of life. They will be able to tap into their own wisdom and feel more empowered by their accountability to truth.

People will put more interest in their dreams, realizing that they are memories of past lives. This will assist them in dreaming more, imagining greater heights, and pouring more creativity into the God stuff of life.

People will realize how the single life mandate has been merely a means of control to prevent them from realizing their own empowerment.

They will be free to cross the veneer between the worlds and visit the great souls who have touched earth with the purest intentions. They will be able to access the greatness in themselves because they will see a greater purpose in sharing one's purpose.

Petty issues and health problems will be less consuming because people won't cling so desperately to this existence as the only chance they get.

The Universe will finally make sense. All the questions of an unfair God will dry up, like why innocent children get sick. It is merely a continuation of a lesson from a past life and not anyone being stricken by a vengeful heartless God.

People will no longer need to think God hates them for what their life entails and realize that if they are not attracting love, happiness, or a partner, that that is something they set in motion somehow in a past life through the taking of a vow or a strong aversion that set in their DNA. That freedom allows them to release whatever is preventing them from having Joy, Love, Abundance, Freedom and Wholeness.

We all come here whole. We are infinite Joy, Love, Abundance, Freedom and Wholeness. If we are not living those things, we realize that there is something in our own experiences that needs to shift. We consume our attention inward instead of throwing rocks at other beings as a form of distraction.

We realize that love is the form of Abundance that we can carry with us lifetime after lifetime. We no longer work so hard to accrue money but innately fall in line with the Spiritual Laws of the Universe so that we can always be rich in the abundance of love.

We stop being enslaved to a linear existence because we realize that a linear world is one of pain, illusion and control.

We stop seeing God as a petty controlling man who wishes to have an ego stroked. Instead, see all of humanity as an atom in the embodiment of God. So anyone who hates any other being in any way, is seen as the hypocrite to God. As the grace of loving others is the true way to show our reverence for God.

52 MESSAGE FROM YOUR HEART

I HOLD YOUR HIGHEST INTENTION

I AM YOUR CONNECTION TO THE DIVINE

I Am the means to offer your prayers up to the Universe

I Am the selling agent that seals the deal with your lover

I Am the gateway to every experience that is worthy of having

When you walk away from me, you are splitting your own effectiveness

I have no ulterior motive but to serve your best interests

I AM your Consigliere

Your confidant

I Am your unflinching, unwavering highest truth

When you betray me, you stray from your ultimate intention

When you ignore me, you ignore your own divinity

I Am the gateway to infinite Love

Devotion is a given

It is not possible to be right and noble while feeling my pang

Others are capable of deceiving you

I AM not

When you ignore my promptings, you ignore all that is sacred in you

You ignore your reason for being here, anywhere

When you listen to another, diminishing my effectiveness

You are diminishing yourself

When you ignore my wisdom, you get fearful

That is when you feel disease

To ease your own pain, turn back to me

Embrace me once again

I am always waiting, always hopeful

That you will acknowledge me once again

And make us whole.

ABOUT THE AUTHOR

Jen Ward is an LMT, a reiki master, shaman, medical intuitive, gifted healer, and an innovator of healing practices. She is at the leading edge of energy work providing an upgrade of understanding of healing from the third dimension to the fifth. She takes the mystery out of what is called faith healing by explaining the physiology behind it in common language. Faith healing is not magic or super powers but merely a heart centered intention manifesting its capabilities. Jen says that there is nothing that a pure intention fueled by a loving heart cannot accomplish.

Humans are so conditioned to come from their mind and this creates the limitations on their abilities. The heart has no limits. Jen explains in the fifth dimension, we are all whole but we have brought with us our engrams (ingrained conditioning) from the third dimension. It is relatively easy for people to release their issues because in the fifth dimension, they are already whole. The work that Jen does is in empowering the individual to realize what they are truly capable of.

Jen is considered a sangoma, a traditional African shaman, who channels ancestors, emoting sounds and vocalizations in ceremonies. An interesting prerequisite to being a sangoma is to have survived the brink of death. When Jen was first approached with the knowledge of being a sangoma, she had not yet fulfilled this prerequisite. However, in April 2008, when she came back to society on the brink of starvation as a result of traumatic involuntary imprisonment, the qualification had been met. She returned to the world of humanity a devout soul inspired to serve.

Her special abilities have also allowed her to innovate a revolutionary technique for finding lost pets by performing an emotional release on the animal. Using this method, she has successfully reunited many lost pets with their owners.

Jen currently works as a long-distance emotional release facilitator, public speaker, and consultant. Her special modality encompasses a holistic overview of her clients from all vantage points, including their physical, emotional, causal, and mental areas, ultimately benefiting their work, home, family, and especially spiritual lives.

You can find Jen here: www.jenuinehealing.com

OTHER BOOKS BY JEN WARD

Enlightenment Unveiled: *Expound into Empowerment.* This book contains case studies to help you peel away the layers to your own empowerment using the tapping technique.

Grow Where You Are Planted: *Quotes for an Enlightened "Jeneration."* Inspirational quotes that are seeds to shift your consciousness into greater awareness.

Perpetual Calendar: *Daily Exercises to Maintain Balance and Harmony in Your Health, Relationships and the Entire World.* 369 days of powerful taps to use as a daily grounding practice for those who find meditation difficult.

Children of the Universe. Passionate prose to lead the reader lovingly into expanded consciousness.

Letters of Accord: *Assigning Words to Unspoken Truth.* Truths that the ancient ones want you to know to redirect your life and humanity back into empowerment.

The Do What You Love Diet: *Finally, Finally, Finally Feel Good in Your Own Skin.* Revolutionary approach to regaining fitness by tackling primal imbalances in relationship to food.

Emerging from the Mist: *Awakening the Balance of Female Empowerment in the World.* Release all the issues that prevent someone from embracing their female empowerment.

Affinity for All Life: *Valuing Your Relationship with all Species.* This book is a means to strengthen and affirm your relationship with the animal kingdom.

The Wisdom of the Trees. If one is struggling for purpose, they can find love, and truth by tuning into the *Wisdom of the Trees.*

Chronicles of Truth. Truth has been buried away for way too long. Here is a means to discover the truth that lies dormant within yourself.

Healing Your Relationships. This book is a means to open up communications and responsiveness to others so that clarity and respect can flourish again in society.

How to Awaken Your Inner Dragon: *Visualizations to Empower Yourself and the World.* Tap into the best possible version of you and the world.

The SFT Lexicon: *Spiritual Freedom Technique.* Tap into the powerful ability of the mind to self heal.

Past Lives, Dreams and Inspiration. People are starving for truth. Unfortunately, they have been conditioned to dismiss their dreams and all remnants of past lives in discovering their own trajectory connection to truth. This book gives life to the expansiveness of self-discovery through one's past lives and dream experiences. There is no greater form of inspiration than discovering one's own depth.

www.ingramcontent.com/pod-product-compliance
Lightning Source LLC
Chambersburg PA
CBHW061648040426
42446CB00010B/1632